RETURN TO HOLLAND

The true spy stories of three brave female secret agents parachuted into Holland to help the Dutch Resistance before Liberation in World War Two.

Bernard O'Connor

Visit my website at
http://www.bernardoconnor.org.uk

ISBN 978-1-901208-36-8

Shortly after moving into the village of Everton in Bedfordshire, UK, I started researching the history of a nearby World War Two airfield. I was very surprised to discover it was where the Special Duties Squadrons flew out on top secret missions to supply the resistance in occupied Europe. As I uncovered more details about the airfield, I published '*RAF Tempsford: Now the Story can be Told*' in 1997. Over the years it has had numerous updates so that the 2010 edition has been renamed '*RAF Tempsford: Churchill's Most Secret Airfield*'.

Interesting, most of the people who bought the book were women. They wanted to find out what their husband, father, grandfather, brother or uncle was doing in the war. In many cases they did not tell them. They were not supposed to. They had signed the Official Secrets Act.

When I was researching the women involved with RAF Tempsford, I discovered over sixty were infiltrated into occupied Europe as secret agents. The vast majority were parachuted into or landed by boat or plane into France; three were parachuted into Belgium and three into Holland. '*The Women of RAF Tempsford: Bedfordshire's TOP SECRET Airfield during World War Two*' tells their stories as well as providing details of those in the Women's Auxiliary Air Force (WAAF) and the First Aid Nursing Yeomanry (FANY), the catering staff and the local women and girls directly and indirectly involved.

Having finished writing up an account of the lives of Elaine Madden, Olga Jackson and Frédérique Dupuich, three women who were parachuted into Belgium on consecutive nights in August 1944, I published '*Return to Belgium*'. I then turned my attention to the stories of Trix Terwindt, Antonia Hamilton and Jos Gemmeke. These equally brave women were parachuted into Holland to liaise with the

Dutch resistance and the invading Allies. I say Holland because the Netherlands was not used by the British War Office or any of its secret services until after World War Two.

Researching the Internet, reading books, magazines and newspaper articles on this period, communicating with people and accessing documents in the National Archives (TNA), I have put together an account of these remarkable women, a story, parts of which may be known to some, that reveal the fascinating behind-the-scenes efforts of the Special Operations Executive (SOE) and the Secret Intelligence Service (SIS) in their plans to expel the German forces occupying Holland.

This period of Holland's history has been exhaustively covered by professional historians but this booklet looks at the role of three women who bravely volunteered to work behind the scenes for their country. Antonia Hamilton, as we shall see, left Holland in the early 1930s but Trix Terwindt and Jos Gemmeke managed to get out during the war and reach England. After being debriefed and specially trained, all three were parachuted back in the early hours of the morning and met with very different experiences. What links they had with RAF Tempsford, what their missions were and how successful they were when they arrived, I have tried to find out.

The role played by the secret services of both Belgium and Holland is comprehensively covered in Airey Neave's *Little Cyclone* and *Saturday at MI9* and in Michael Foot's *The SOE in the Low Countries'.* Whilst interviews with 'Trix' Terwindt appeared in the Dutch media after the war and the story of Jos Gemmeke has been told by Eddy de Roever in *Sphinx*, it has not been translated into English. Antonia Hamilton's story has not been published. The episode on 'The Dutch Disaster' on Athena's 2011 documentary TV series and the History Channel's 'Spying Game' provided valuable additional detail based on interviews with some of the men and women involved. This account also uses the women's recently released personnel files in the National Archives and other sources to tell their stories.

In order to write about these remarkable women and others involved in the Dutch resistance, I would like to acknowledge the assistance of the staff at the National Archives in Kew, London, John Clinch, Philippe Connart, Rien Emmery, Thomas Ensminger, Lex Goumare, Steven Kippax, Frans Kluiters, Lieven Saerens, Luc Vanhaverbeke, Xavier Van Tilborg, Kim Steenberg, Reijer Vaarkamp and the following websites: 64-Baker Street, belgiumww2, Comète line, dbnl (bibliotheek voor de Nederlandse letteren), historylearningsite, Spartacus, the specialoperationsexecutive user group on yahoo.com, verzetmuseum and Wikipedia.

Following Hitler's armed forces success in capturing Czechoslovakia and Poland in 1939 and invading Denmark and Norway in April 1940, on 10 May, the Whitsun holiday when governments were in recess, he ordered the *Sichelschnitt,* a military attack on France, Luxembourg, Belgium and Holland.

The German armies pushed through to the North Sea coast within days but not quick enough to stop the British warship HMS *Hereward,* sent by King George VI with the orders to rescue Queen Wilhelmina, her family and her Government and bringing them to safety in the UK. They were offered accommodation and facilities which including broadcasting time on the BBC as Radio Oranje. Following the announcement of their surrender on 15 May, few Dutch citizens had the opportunity to escape. They had to come to terms with living under occupation.

Hitler's threat to annihilate Rotterdam and every other Dutch city unless they surrendered worked. Holland was to become Germany's market garden. Other plans included utilising Dutch as well as Belgian airfields from where the Luftwaffe could attack Britain. Some Dutch factories were taken over for Germany's war effort. Thousands of able-bodied Dutch men were taken to work in Germany's industries as forced labour under the '*Arbeitseinsatz*' scheme whilst the German men were in the Wehrmacht. Securing transport routes across northwest Europe, particularly from the Atlantic and North Sea ports, was another aim.

In terms of helping the people of Holland, Great Britain found itself in a difficult situation when the Germans invaded. In the summer of 1940 the SIS, Secret Intelligence Service, the clandestine section of the British Foreign Office, approached the Air Ministry with

The War Office, Whitehall, London, where Airey Neave and James Langley made decisions about helping the Dutch resistance and sent messages to SOE's N Section in Baker Street for action.

(http://upload.wikimedia.org/wikipedia/commons/7/7f/Old_war_office.jpg 27 October 2009)

Norgeby House, 83 Baker Street, London, where SOE's Dutch Section had their Headquarters 1941-45.

www.bca.uk.com/viewcentre.aspx?cid=983 27 October 2009

the suggestion that they experiment in how feasible it would be to parachute agents and land aircraft to pick up stranded troops and VIPs (Very Important Persons). They felt that they could be more useful for the war effort if they were in Britain. Many persons of great value to England and her allies had been left behind when the Germans overran France and the Low Countries. Some key trained individuals deliberately stayed behind and merged into the local population to help encourage and clandestinely train those who them opposed the German assimilation of the conquered territories.

It was essential that some of these people needed occasionally bringing back to England for additional training and then sent back to the resistance groups. The urgency of the situation was taken on board and the Special Operations Executive (SOE) was born. Their operations were to be 'unattributable' industrial sabotage, the raising and supplying of secret armies and collecting intelligence information, all done under what Michael Foot, the SOE historian, describes as '*the dense fog of secrecy*'.

To hide their true purposes, SOE's Headquarters were in a five floor office block at 64 Baker Street, in Marylebone, Westminster. A brass plate outside the door read 'Inter-Services Research Bureau'. Those in the know called it 'The Organisation', 'The Org' or 'The Firm'. As it had to have War Department cover its letters were headed with the name M.O.I. (S.P.) and its telephone number added to the War Office's directory. Captain Peter Lee, an officer in its security section, said "*it was terribly clever. We said it stood for 'Mysterious Operations in Special Places'. We reckoned the Germans, with their lack of sense of humour, would never be able to unravel that one.*"

The SOE had largely been the brainchild of Dr Hugh Dalton, the Minister for Economic Warfare. It was his intention that it would be used as a 'Fourth Arm' or 'Secret Army' and undertake all forms of irregular warfare. Winston Churchill is said to have thought that this Fourth Arm would "Set Europe Ablaze!"

Each country where the SOE was to operate was given a letter. The Dutch section, known as N, had offices in Norgeby House, 83 Baker Street. It was inaugurated on 20 December 1940 under the control of Mr R. V. Laming, who before the war had been a commercial counsellor in The Hague.

Foot pointed out that N Section had problems at the outset. Laming had been in conflict with Francois van 't Sant, the Chief of Police in The Hague, over an incident before the war but he had had to acquiesce as 't Sant had Queen Wilhelmina's friendship and support. In fact, she appointed him as her trusted Minister of Security with headquarters in offices on Chester Street in London. However, these differences had to be overcome as it was through the SOE that most of the Dutch agents were trained and dispatched into Holland

Dutch-speaking Major Charles Blizard, codename 'Blunt', was recruited from Military Intelligence to take over as head of N Section on 19 December 1941. He was replaced by Seymour Bingham on 24 February 1943 and R. I. Dobson took over in late February 1944 and ran the section until the end of the war. (Foot, op.cit. pp.82-6) They will appear later on in the account.

According to Foot, one of the first women to join N section was Sybil Bond, a second subaltern in the

Wanborough Manor, near Guildford, Surrey, where potential Dutch agents were assessed as to their suitability for clandestine activity.

http://www.violetteszabo.org/images/275_WanboroughManor_GrdTallBldg_04Jul04.JPG

Arisaig House, one of the secluded hunting lodges in Northwest Scotland, where Dutch and other agents were trained in the art of 'ungentlemanly warfare'.

http://media.photobucket.com/image/arisaig%20soe/Section1/swiki/a1/

Dunham House, Cheshire, where agents were accommodated whilst they had their parachute training at nearby Ringway airport, near Manchester.

http://farm1.static.flickr.com/12/16413226_857f970399.jpg

Beaulieu Abbey, Hampshire, SOE's 'Finishing School' where agents were given intensive training in clandestine operations. They lived in large houses within the grounds of the estate.
http://koti.welho.com/rhurmal1/linnat2004/img0007.jpg

Auxiliary Territorial Service. Blizard left his wife and married Sybil, a woman many years younger than himself and she remained in the section

> *...till the end of the war; earning golden opinions for her conscientious work from her last section head. Her original duties were hardly more than clerical, but she came to take over the business of allotting prospective agents to training courses and preparing them to go to the field; and it was largely to her that the gloomy task fell of taking dead agents' belongings back to their families after the war. After marriage, she continued to use her maiden name at work.* (Foot, op.cit)

Their only secretary was Elsie French. According to Foot, she spoke perfect Dutch having been born in The Hague of British parents and brought up bilingual. Before the SOE requisitioned office space in Michael House, another office block on Baker Street, she had worked as one of Marks and Spencer's clerks. When she was eighteen she joined SOE, worked devotedly hard and pleased everybody, going on after the war to work with Prince Bernhard's staff.

Choosing agents to send into Holland on clandestine missions was the task of Selwyn Jepson. Initially interviews were held in a room at the Northumberland Hotel, near Baker Street, but from late-1943 all SOE agents and field operatives underwent psychological screening at Stodham Park, (Special Training School (STS 3) ,a 19 century country house near Liss in Hampshire. This was to reduce the drop-out rate later in training and failures in the field. After interviews, N's potential secret agents had to sign what was called 'The Poison Book', the Official Secrets Act. They were not to divulge anything about their work to anybody outside what was called 'The Organisation', 'The Org', 'The Racket' or 'The Firm'.

Where exactly they were recruited from was not mentioned. Most were probably people from the military, business or education communities who had been in England before the war or who had managed to get out down one of the escape lines. One of the major requirements would have been able that they were able to speak Dutch. Being able to speak French and/or German would have been an advantage.

Some of those who signed 'The Poison Book', told nobody about their war-time work and took their stories to the grave. Those who talked to newspaper reporters or attempted to publish their wartime memoirs or autobiographies after the war, had to have their work purged of sensitive information by the government. Over time, as those involved died and biographers and historians have had access to their personal files, more light has been shed on what went on behind the scenes in these secret organisations.

The next stage was at Winterfold (STS 4), a large country house at the foot of the Surrey Hills near Cranleigh, between Guildford and Horsham. They were given a rail pass to Guildford where a tarpaulin covered truck would pick them up from the station forecourt and take them to the school. They were not supposed to be able to identify its location.

After July 1943 Winterfold became STS 7, where more formal "student assessments" were done. Whilst undergoing training, 'students' were given a pseudonym and told not to divulge their true identity or much about their background to anyone. Their instructors would all have spoken Dutch and the other students in their group would all have been Dutch. As well as physical training they were given rope work, weapons training, lessons in Morse Code, map work, orienteering and psychological and other assessment tests. They may have overheard people speaking Belgian or other European languages but not French.

Agents destined for France went to the 16 century Wanborough Manor, Puttenham, at the foot of the Hog's Back ridge near Guildford, set in a 1,766 acre estate. There was no rationing in these centres. Students could eat and drink as much as they liked but, their 'accompanying'. 'escorting' or 'conducting officer' made careful note on how they behaved, even their table manners. They were encouraged to drink, but if they got drunk and talked too much about their real life or were too critical of the system, they would fail. Unsuitable candidates went back to normal work, none the wiser about the real work of SOE. A few days leave in London or back home was probably very welcome.

Trix, Antonia and Jos, in all likelihood, would have understood Nancy Wake's description of Winterfold as 'The Mad House'. The types of exercises they were given made many 'students' wonder at the reasons behind them. Obstacle courses were laid out with various objects like tyres, nets, logs and barrels were set out and labelled A, B and C. One student might be told to climb over all the As, go clockwise round the Bs and anticlockwise round the Cs whilst a second student had to go clockwise round the As, go clockwise round the Bs and climb over the Cs. Other tasks included using whatever means they could to cross a large pond without getting their feet wet, traversing a large wooden frame without letting their feet touching the ground and group work carrying full water butts across a lawn without spilling any. There were memory games where they were shown a tray with dozens of objects which they had to memorise. The tray was then taken away and one item removed and, when it was brought back, students had to identify which item was missing. They might be given a photograph to study and then be asked to describe in detail what was in it. Someone was brought into the class; they had to study them and, when they had gone, a detailed description of them had to be given.

What puzzled many were the psychological tests. They were taken into an office, sat down and shown an assortment of ink blots on cards which, spontaneously, they had to suggest what shapes they resembled. Their responses were written down. Presumably, their answers shed light on their personality. Once the 'assessment' was finished they were returned home to await a decision.

Those assessed as being suitable material were notified by post or telephone and sent a rail pass with a note to rendezvous at Euston Station in London. There they would meet their conducting officer and board the night train to Edinburgh from where they changed for Fort William and Arisaig, a remote estate in Inverness-shire on the northwest coast of Scotland. Here they were accommodated in one of eleven shooting lodges for three or four weeks paramilitary training, what was called 'the art of ungentlemanly warfare', The courses included yet more physical training, silent killing, weapons handling, grenade throwing, knife work, rope work, boat work, demolition of railway engines, railway lines and bridges, map reading, compass work, field craft (outdoor survival), more Morse code, burglary, key cutting, forgery, learning how to jump off moving trains and advanced raid tactics.

Like at Winterfold, there was no rationing, the diet being augmented by freshly caught fish, crab, mackerel, mussels and oysters. Occasionally a hand grenade tossed into a river might have killed a salmon or a good shot with a rifle brought down a deer. The local hotel and pubs were not off-limits and bottles of whisky were not in short supply.

Their instructors and conducting officer wrote reports on their skill and aptitude, recommending whether they were suitable for clandestine work. Those who failed this course were sent to 'The Cooler', a remote country estate at Inverlair, where they made mountaineering equipment for the duration of the war. What they had learned had not to be revealed to the general public until it was deemed safe for them to be 'released'. And then, having signed the Official Secrets Act, they would be expected to 'keep mum', tell no-one.

After a farewell party to which many girls from outlying villages and fishing ports were brought in, the agents caught the train to Manchester. Again trucks were arranged to take them to their next course, parachute training at Ringway Airfield (STS 51), about twelve miles (25 km) south of Manchester.

During the time they spent there, up a week depending on the weather, they were accommodated either at Dunham House (STS 51a), near Altrincham, Fulshaw Hall (STS 51b), near Wilmslow, or York House (STS 51c), near Timperley. To get their 'wings' they had to complete at least three drops from an air balloon and two from an airplane into the grounds of the adjoining estate of Tatton Park. At least one drop was at night. Once the course was completed they were given a few days leave in London.

The 'Finishing School' was at Beaulieu, the 8,000 estate of Lord Montagu in the New Forest, close to Bournemouth on the South Coast. It had had seven requisitioned, large country houses hidden away in the park where the 'students' stayed. No wonder many agents described the SOE as standing for 'Stately 'Omes of England'. As well as more physical training, students were taught the art of fieldcraft, use of British and enemy weapons as well as specialist classes in 'spycraft', identifying enemy uniforms, avoiding detection, breaking and entering, forgery and disguises. They were even given experience of withstanding Gestapo interrogation.

Some days they were sent into Southampton or Bournemouth with a mission to undertake. It might be to rendezvous with someone, pass on a message, find out information, catch a particular train, jump out at a particular point and report back to the house before a particular time, all the while ensuring that they weren't followed. They had to learn from their mistakes.

The Dutch men would have been approached by particularly attractive women, specially chosen to test the agents' suitability for clandestine work. After a good meal and plenty of alcohol they might be invited to bed and subtly questioned as to what exercises they had been doing, who the other students were and what their teachers were like. If their pillow talk let slip 'sensitive' information, they would fail the course. There is no evidence suggesting that Trix, Antonia, Jos or any of the other women agents, had attractive men try and seduce information out of them.

Some women reported that they were not allowed spirits whilst at Beaulieu but drinking local beer was common. One group, when last orders was called, was said to have had forty pints lined up along the counter in the bar and not being allowed to go to sleep until they had all been drunk. Woe betide anyone who was awoken in the night and was not talking Dutch. All the lessons were in Dutch; the reading material was in Dutch and they even listened to Radio Oranje.

Before they finished the course they were given a two or three day 'schedule' where they had to visit a town or city, sometimes a long distance away, identify suitable 'safe' houses, choose dead letter boxes, maybe break into a building, steal or photograph documents and rendezvous with contacts, all the time ensuring that they were never followed.

There was training in getting on and off Lysander and Hudson airplanes for those who were not going to be parachuted in. Those whose job might include training reception committees in parachute drops or landings needed to learn how to arrange the lights for the flarepath.

Depending on the type of specialist training the SOE, SIS or the OSS, American Office of Strategic Services, deemed necessary for their agents to have, they were sent to one of a number of specialist training schools.

Agents sent to Gumley Hall (STS 44), an 18 century mansion near Market Harborough in Leicestershire, with forty-five bedrooms set in 2,000 acres, received intensive weapons training and further unarmed combat lessons under the command of Major J. H. Drumbell. Those destined for industrial sabotage work went to the 17 Brickendonbury Manor (STS 17), near Hertford in Hertfordshire. Initially under the command of Captain Frederic Thomas and then by Colonel George Rheam, students were taught exactly which part of a factory, power station, telephone exchange, railway, dock or shipyard to target, exactly where to place the explosives, what quantities to use and which type of time pencil - the half hour, one hour, two hour or longer.

Those identified as potential wireless or radio operators were sent to Thame Park (STS 52), in Oxfordshire for intensive wireless and security training using the most up-to-date equipment. The SOE 'boffins' were constantly improving radio communications technology. Agents had to be able to type messages in Morse Code at between eighteen and twenty-two words per minute, to encode and decipher messages accurately and use appropriate safety checks in their transmissions to let headquarters know they were still safe. Missing them out would indicate they were operating under duress or that someone else was typing. As we shall see, this was a very serious problem for the Dutch section's agents.

Some might have been sent to Howbury Hall (STS 40), near Bedford, where they would have been given specialist training in using Eureka, Rebecca and S-Phones, the latest ground-to-air communication equipment.

During their briefing sessions for their missions, agents stayed in houses or flats rented by N section in and around London. They visited the dentist to ensure they only had Dutch fillings. They were provided with Dutch clothes, given Dutch haircuts and kept up-to-date with news from Holland, the latest films, radio programmes, curfew times, ration cards and other permits needed so as not to give anyone the impression that they had just arrived from England. They had to fit seamlessly back into normal society. They had to write their will and letters and postcards to loved ones that would be sent at designated times throughout their 'absence'. Their 'conducting officer' would also go over their cover story, the role they had to adopt back in Holland, and carefully examine photographs and maps of the 'drop zone'.

Once fully briefed as to their mission, agents were kept until the flight was ready at what were called 'Holding Stations' or 'Holding Schools'. Here they were provided with high class 'Rest and Recreation'. There were no holds barred except, as far as I can determine, sex and drugs. The Dutch agents were probably accommodated with the Belgians at the 18 Chicheley Hall (STS 20) near Newport Pagnell in Buckinghamshire, described as one of England's finest and loveliest English country houses. Other nationalities were taken to West Court (STS 6), a fine 17 century mansion at Finchampstead Lea, near Reading in Berkshire, Audley End (STS 43), near Hertford or the closest one, Gaynes Hall (STS 61), near St Neots which was less than an hour's drive from RAF Tempsford.

What might now be called 'Rest and Recreation' was provided by attractive young women in the FANY. Fine food and wine, dancing, chatting, playing games of ping pong or cards and listening to the wireless might while away the hours whilst they waited. Two eggs on their plate was the unwritten message that their mission was on that night. A blacked-out car would arrive after dinner and the FANY would drive the agent and their conducting officer to the airfield which would be ready to take them to Holland.

The 419 Squadron, who undertook these missions on behalf of the SOE were initially based on the Heath near Newmarket Racecourse, about 14 miles (22.4 kms.) east of Cambridge. Their twin-engined Armstrong Whitworth Whitley bombers and Wellington IIIs had to be specially converted to carry, not bombs, but supplies for the resistance as well as parachutists who would be dropped in the early hours of the morning on moonlit nights. Pilots had to learn how to fly low and without lights.

In October 1941, once John Laing, the construction company working at Tempsford, had prepared the three runways, the flight was transferred. Two Special Duties Squadrons were formed. 161 Squadron had responsibilities for landing and picking up operations and 138 Squadron undertook the dropping of supplies and agents.

Leo Marks, Head of SOE's code section during WW2 holding up a silk sheet on which the agent's code was printed. His book *Between Silk and Cyanide* tells of his wartime experiences with the Dutch Section.

http://t1.gstatic.com/images?q=tbn:sM4ZJ6zDuqK-iM:http://www.mishalov.com/images/

Francois van 't Sant, head of Dutch Secret Police in the Hague and, following the invasion, in offices in Chester Street, London. Seen here on Pall Mall, near St James' Palace.

http://nl.wikipedia.org/wiki/Bestand:Fran%C3%A7oisvantSant.jpg

Seymour Bingham, Head of SOE's N Section during WW2. Based in offices in Norgeby House, 83 Baker Street from 24 February 1943.

http://uk.groups.yahoo.com/group/specialoperationsexecutive/photos/album/468430941/pic/736373400/view?picmode=&mode=tn&order=ordinal&start-1&count=20&dir=asc

R. I. Dobson took over as Head of N Section from Major Charles Blizard in early 1944 and managed the office until the end of the war.

http://uk.groups.yahoo.com/group/specialoperationsexecutive/photos/album/468430941/pic/736373400/view?picmode=&mode=tn&order=ordinal&start=1&count=20&dir=asc

Colonel David J. Keswick, SOE's Regional Controller of NW Europe, codename at Baker Street was D/R.

http://uk.groups.yahoo.com/group/specialoperationsexecutive/photos/album/468430941/pic/736373400/view?picmode=&mode=tn&order=ordinal&start=1&count=20&dir=asc

Tempsford was a small agricultural village on the A1 about fifty miles (80 kms.) north of London, in a remote area roughly half way between Cambridge and Bedford, The airfield was sited on specially drained clay land between the main railway line between London and Edinburgh and the Greensand Ridge to the east. Many who were stationed there thought it was the boggiest and foggiest in England.

Because of the top secret nature of their work, the airfield had been designed by a magician. To be more accurate, Jasper Maskelyne was an illusionist who had entertained in London theatres before the war. It was built to resemble a disused airfield. Some of the farm labourers' cottages and farm buildings were demolished. The roof slates of Gibraltar Farm were removed to make it look derelict. Windows had the glass deliberately broken. Sacks were draped across the inside of the windows instead of curtains. The doors were left rickety. For the same reason much of the black Bedfordshire weather-boarding was removed. The adjacent farm buildings got the same treatment and visitors reported them being mildewed, cobwebbed and covered in mouldering thatch. Some locals suggest that tarpaulins were draped over hangars and new buildings on which agricultural buildings had been painted.

Inside Gibraltar Farm it was said that the stairs, ceiling and first floor were removed to create a very large room. The inside walls were built up and reinforced to withstand bomb damage. This was to be the airfield's nerve centre. All the hangars and domestic buildings were camouflaged to blend in with the surrounding farmland and some were said to have been thatched - to give the impression that they were farm buildings. Nissen huts resembled pig sties or cow sheds.

Outside Gibraltar Farm the pond was left with the odd few ducks. Genuine tractors were left but moved

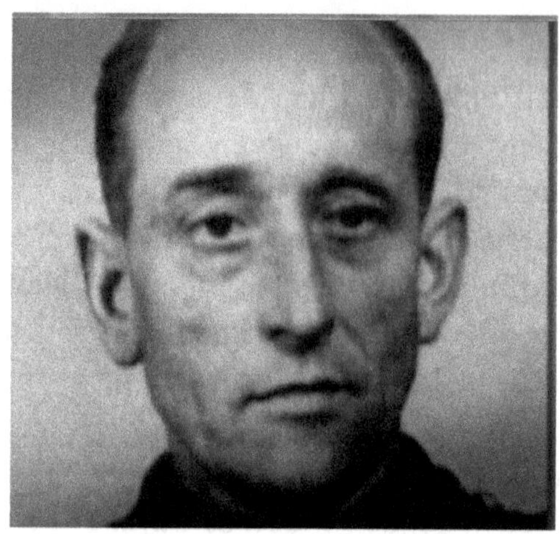

Major Charles Blizard, Head of N Section until the discovery of the Englandspiel

(DVD 'Secret War - Episode 7 The Dutch Disaster', Athena, 2011)

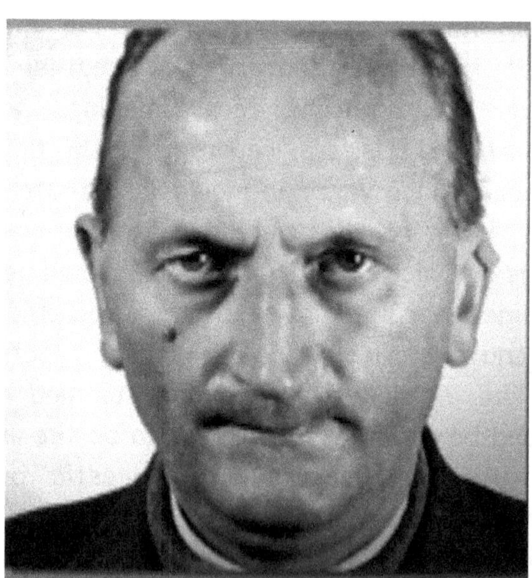

Obersleutenant Hermann J. Giskes, Chief of the Abwehr III/F counter-espionage operation in Holland and Belgium, who ran the Englandspiel.

(DVD 'Secret War - Episode 7 The Dutch Disaster', Athena, 2011)

Major General Colin Gubbins, Head of the SOE at the time of the Englandspiel

(DVD 'Secret War - Episode 7 The Dutch Disaster', Athena, 2011)

The Catholic seminary at Haaren in the south of Holland, requisitioned by the Germans and used to imprison Trix Terwindt and other captured Dutch agents.

(DVD 'Secret War - Episode 7 The Dutch Disaster', Athena, 2011)

occasionally in the fields and yards. The runways were painted grey and green in places to look like they were overgrown. At one point a thick black line was painted across the runway, to give overflying pilots the impression that it was the continuation of a hedge. Cattle were deliberately grazed on some of the fields when the runways were not in use to make the pilots of any German planes that managed to fly over think it was used for agricultural purposes. It succeeded. Even though over two thousand personnel were based there it is said that the aerial photographs taken by German pilots who flew over were interpreted as a disused airfield. The local people knew there was an airfield there but they were not allowed access during the nights between the waxing and waning moon. They never knew what went on down the hill. They were not supposed to.

Once established at what became known as 'Tempsford Station', other planes were brought into use including the much larger Short Stirling and the Handley Page Halifax bomber for parachute drops and Hudsons and Lysanders for landing and pick-ups. The latter had to be modified to carry secret agents to fields within a five hundred mile (800 kms.) or so distance from the English coast. Consequently, there were no Lysander missions to Holland, only Hudsons. Once they got out with their luggage, special passengers climbed in. These included V.I.Ps , military personnel, politicians, industrialists, resistance leaders and secret agents who had been in the field and needed bringing back. It was not uncommon for women agents to be sent out and, if they evaded capture, brought back. Other women passengers like wives and girlfriends of influential politicians, industrialists and resistance figures, were exfiltrated. Details of their

Airey Neave,
MI9's coordinator of escape and evasion organisation, helped finance and support the escape lines from Holland, through Belgium, France, Switzerland, Spain, Portugal back to Britain.

http://www.tremele.nl/Oorlog/wo2/05regimenten/LeoHeaps/AireyNeave_young.jpg

Trix Terwindt
Worked with Dutch resistance when war broke out, escaped into Belgium in March 1942 and travelled through France, Switzerland, Spain and Portugal before reaching England in August. Trained as an agent, code-named Felix, she was parachuted back into Holland on 13th February 1943, arrested, interrogated and imprisoned.

http://www.gelderlander.nl/multimedia/archive/00837/trixterwindt_837305b.jpg

Jos Gemmeke

Helped print and deliver underground paper *Je Maintiendrai* and helped carry radio sets and other equipment for SOE agents. Cycled to Belgium in October 1944 to deliver microfiche to Prince Bernhard, flown to England, trained by SOE and parachuted back into Holland on 10 March 1945. Codenamed *Sphinx* and known as *Els von Dalen.*, she worked with the Resistance and was awarded the *Militaire Willemsorde.*

http://www.onderscheidingenforum.nl/viewtopic.php?f=24&t=776

Jos Gemmeke receiving her *Militaire Willemsorde* from Queen Wilhelmina in appreciation of the contribution she made to the Dutch resistance.

boekje-pienter.eu/images/canon-jos_gemmeke02.jpg

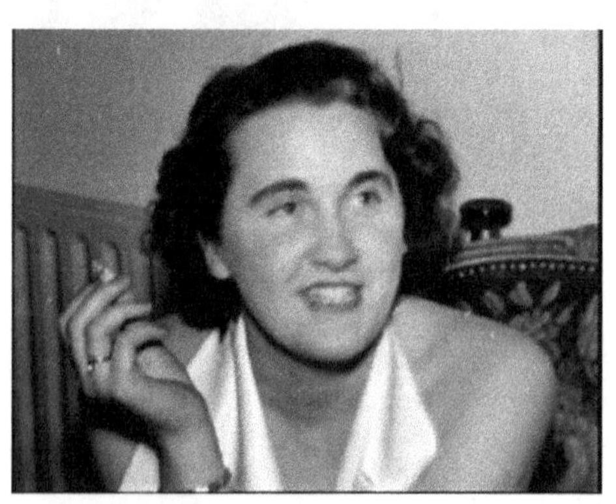

Jos Gemmeke in a more leisurely role.

(Clip from 'The Spying Game, History Channel, 2007)

stories can be found in Bernard O'Connor's "*'The Women of RAF Tempsford.*"

The first batch of Dutch agents was named after vegetables, the next after games and the last after loud noises. The names given to the three women focussed on in this work were Chicory, Tiddlywinks and Cackle. Those readers who know about the Dutch resistance, will understand the huge problems that these agents faced. Britain's pre-war Allied information network in Holland had been effectively destroyed in November 1939 through the successful penetration by the Abwehr, the German Security Office. Two British intelligence officers, Captain Payne Best and Colonel Stevens, had been captured in what became known as the 'Venlo incident'.

There was suspicion of the motives of some of the immigrants arriving in Britain. Richard Deacon, the military historian, commented that

> *The most dangerous of these refugees were the Dutch ...* (who) *are notorious for producing double agents and treacherous agents. It may seem unkind and even unjust to make so sweeping an allegation against a whole nation, but, though the Dutch are often perfectly delightful, peaceful, honest citizens, when it comes to espionage they are thoroughly unreliable, with few exceptions. It should have been obvious to S.O.E. executives that there were many secret Nazi sympathisers among these Dutch refugees, just as in the ranks of the Dutch Resistance movement in Holland were many Nazi agents. But for some reason the policy-makers decided to speed up their attempts to develop an*

> *operationally effective Dutch section of S.O.E. before all others.* (Deacon, R. *A History of the British Secret Service,* Muller, (1969), p.299)

Dropping agents and supplies into Holland was not as easy as it was into larger countries like France, Norway or Poland. Foot identified a number of problems that the SOE experienced with Holland. In the first few years of the war there was a shortage of available aircraft. The RAF was unwilling to allocate large numbers of planes to secret operations with the threat of German invasion and the importance of bombing missions. There were few remote areas in Holland where Tempsford pilots could safely drop agents and containers of supplies without being seen.

Once agents had been dropped, there was the difficulty of safe movement within the country when there were so many places where the Germans had controls, especially at the innumerable bridges over the rivers, canals and dikes. Perhaps the worst problem was pilots having to fly low over one of the world's heaviest concentrations of anti-aircraft gun emplacements. In fact, the Special Duties Squadrons experienced so many losses over Holland that they curtailed all flights there in May 1943. We shall see why their fears were justified later.

Apart from the pressures of time, human problems were also identified by Foot. There was poor co-ordination between N Section and the shifting Dutch authorities in charge of irregular warfare. As has been mentioned, Francois van 't Sant, Queen Wilhelmina's head of *Centrale Inlichtingsdienst*, the first Dutch intelligence service in exile, and Laming, the first head of N Section, had no time for each other. There were also conflicts of interest between the SOE and the SIS. They were concerned that acts of sabotage interfered with their quieter, more covert methods working behind the scenes as well as the Foreign Office sometimes having to deal with the repercussions of SOE activities. It needs to be remembered that the existence of both these agencies was denied by the British establishment. This was TOP SECRET work.

There was a lack of understanding by both the British and the Dutch secret services about what life was really like in Holland. Most of their officials came from the middle and upper classes who had either left Holland before the war or escaped during the invasion. This hampered the choice of targets and the choice of the right equipment necessary for the jobs. Foot also suggests that many of the agents sent over were 'not of the highest calibre'. Too many, he argues, did not follow their SOE instructions or training and succumbed much too easily and too early to sophisticated interrogation techniques used by the Germans.

Whilst the SIS had sent in six agents between 27 August 1940 and 16 August 1941 only two were still active. One had drowned, two had been shot and one was in prison. SOE's first mission was what Blizard called the 'Plan for Holland'. On the night of 7/8 November 1941 Flight Lieutenant Murphy of 1419 Squadron, took off from Newmarket racecourse in Suffolk, flew across the North Sea and crossed the Dutch coast about eight miles (15 km) north of Ijmuiden at a height of only 100 feet. Just after midnight, Thijs Taconis, a trained saboteur, and his wireless operator, Hubertus Lauwers were parachuted into Holland having been warned that theirs was a dangerous mission. They had to organise and galvanise the Dutch Resistance into acts of sabotage.

Once Lauwers informed SOE of a drop zone not far from Arnhem where Taconis was living, on 6/7 March 1942 Pilot Officer Russell took off from Tempsford, the Special Duties Squadron's new airfield, in Bedfordshire. He flew to the Hindeloopen area of Holland where he dropped six containers and six packages straight into German hands. The SOE was unaware that Lauwers, codenamed EBENEEZER, had been captured and was transmitting under duress.

Taconis had gone to Arnhem to set up an SOE circuit and recruited a diamond smuggler who promised him a truck to pick up the containers. What he did not know was that this man was a V-Manner, the term used for a police informer, who sold intelligence to Obersleutenant Hermann J. Giskes, the Chief of the Abwehr III/F counter-espionage operation in Holland and Belgium. On being told that the German navy cruiser, Prinz Eugen, was going to be in Scheidam docks for repairs, Taconis needed a message sent urgently to London. Giskes ordered his wireless detection team to listen for any illegal broadcasts, which led to Lauwers' arrest at his wireless set on 6 March and the collection of the containers. Three ciphered texts were found containing the code he was using to transmit to London. Under torture and threat of execution, he agreed to work for the Germans under the control of Giskes. (DVD 'Secret War - Episode 7 The Dutch Disaster', Athena, 2011)

Having been thoroughly trained in England before he was dropped, Lauwers deliberately sent his messages back to London without the correct security checks, hoping that it might provide a clue that the operation was compromised. He had to deliberately mis-spell the sixteenth letter or a multiple of sixteen. However, when he didn't and despite inserting the letters CAU and GHT as often as he could among the jumbled letters which normally preceded and terminated each message. He mis-spelt stop as step to suggest he was compromised but the signal that came back read 'INSTRUCT NEW OPERATOR IN USE OF SECURITY CHECK'. He had been exposed. Threatened with execution, he agreed to transmit Giskes' messages to London. Although his messages were stamped 'Security Check omitted, when Blizard took over, he decided that it was just Lauwers making a mistake. (Ibid.)

So began what Giskes described as *Der Englandspiel* and later '*Operation Nordpol*'. Between 1942 and 1944 the Germans made arrangements for the SOE to send in more than fifty agents, supplies and money straight into their hands. Chris Burton writing in *Air Power History* pointed out how else their operation was so successful. A month after the war ended, Major General Sir Colin Gubbins, the then head of SOE, asked the head of the OSS in Washington to search its collection of captured enemy documents for information relating to Germany's wartime knowledge of SOE or OSS secret operations. His

> ... *postwar inquiries into SOE's Holland disaster confirmed what may have been suspected -yet not circulated throughout the special operations community - that as early as 1942 the Germans had captured and activated Eureka beacons in order to manipulate Allied DZs. Due to these gaps in* operational *security, Allied commands continued to issue Eureka beacons throughout the war without modifications that would limit their vulnerability to further enemy exploitation.*
>
> *More than sixty years later, historical assessments of enemy technical countermeasures to Allied special operations tend to concentrate on German Funkspiele or "radio games," that often deceived Allied special operations headquarters through the playback of captured agent radio transmitters. This paper builds*

> *upon that premise and suggests that, in certain cases, German manipulation of the Allies' Eureka-Rebecca system could not only in theory produce an effective countermeasure, but could also compromise an important layer of Allied security and provide Berlin the initial, technical capability to infiltrate Allied special operations. German manipulation of Eureka-Rebecca could theoretically simulate special operations DZs to establish a trap for the capture of Allied personnel, and to help provide a foundation for the subsequent radio games whose devastating impact ended so many clandestine operations.* (http://vlex.com/vid/eureka-rebecca-compromises-operations-ii-56727120)

It was Leo Marks, SOE's code master, who first suspected in January 1943 that something was wrong. In his autobiography '*Between Silk and Cyanide*' he acknowledged that about 20% of wireless operators' messages contained mistakes, which the girls at Grendon Underwood, SOE's receiving station, had to try and decipher. As the traffic from Holland contained no 'indecipherables', he deduced that they were being sent by German experts. To confirm his fears, Marks sent them an indecipherable. When they didn't complain, he knew they were German. Trying to prove it to Maurice Buckmaster proved impossible, making some Dutch commentators believe that the upper echelons of the SOE were aware of the game being played by the Germans. They argue that the SOE deliberately kept on supplying the Germans with agents and stores in the belief that it would distract their attention away from the Allies' true intentions for D-Day. Foot emphatically denied it. Marks' final proof came when he instructed one of the wireless operators to transmit a message to Holland concluding it with the Morse

Code letters HH. The immediate reply came back HH, Heil Hitler. It was a German operator. He explained his belief that the entire Dutch network was compromised. went to see Major General Colin Gubbins, the Head of SOE. And was told not to discuss it with anyone else. Although Blizard was transferred to a desk job in the War Office on 24 February 1943 and replaced by Seymour Bingham, agents continued to be dropped into Holland. Nine sent in March, April and May 1943 were caught and imprisoned. (Marks, L. *Between Silk and Cyanide,* Harper Collins (1998); DVD 'Secret War - Episode 7 The Dutch Disaster', Athena, 2011)

Accounts of this double-cross or double-double-cross have been published in other books. Max Hastings, the war historian, in an article in the *Daily Mail* entitled 'Winston Churchill the Terrorist' claimed that the revelation of SOE's Dutch disaster precipitated a crisis. Their opponents in Whitehall began to demand that it curtailed its operations and calls for resources. It was accused of rank amateurishness and lack of tradecraft which had led to a severe cost in life and wasted effort. Some wanted SOE disbanded but Churchill refused. He was not going to be deflected from his pet project. He renewed SOE's mandate, arguing that its enthusiasm and activism far outweighed its deficiencies. Instead of scaling down SOE's activities, he ordered the RAF to provide the Special Duties Squadrons with more aircraft for arms-dropping operations. Bingham who had been tricked by Giskes, was sent to a post in Australia. Blizard, who had also been tricked and sent in forty agents, escaped any blame.

Michael Foot, the official SOE historian, asserts in his *SOE in the Low Countries*, that it was incompetence, not perfidy, that brought on this debacle. Jo Walters, author of *Dossier Nordpol* and *Englandspiel SOE's Worst Wartime*

Disaster, suggests that there was a 'purposeful policy' by some British authority, other than SOE's Dutch Section, whereby Dutch agents were deployed as 'shock troops', deliberately to keep as many German troops as possible in the West in 1942 to relieve the pressures on the Russians during Operation Barbarossa, when three German army groups invaded the Soviet Union. Needless to say, there are still strong feelings about it today.

It is worth mentioning that in Probert and Cox's *The Battle Re-Thought* they state that the German listening services often heard 138 squadron aircraft - of which they recognised the R/T call signals - talking to Tempsford flying control on afternoon test flights, and were able to forewarn the Abwehr that there might be clandestine aircraft activity that night. The Germans knew from their wireless communications with London exactly when the Tempsford planes were due to arrive. They duly informed the Luftwaffe night fighter forces based at Driebergen and Gilze-Rijen to be on the look-out as well as the men staffing the formidable barrage of anti-aircraft batteries along the coast. Although not documented, it is likely they were ordered to shoot them down once the 138 Squadron pilots had dropped their agents and canisters. Even as late as September 1942, pilots were ordered to wink their navigation light several times when they identified the narrow triangle of three lights on the ground.

The Secret War's episode on 'The Dutch Disaster' claims that it was the RAF that finally halted the Englandspiel. Pilots reported five times more losses of planes and aircrew over Holland than what was expected. German night fighters appeared to be waiting for them where none ought to have been. Navigators reported the lights at the DZs being too perfectly lit. In November 1943, Bomber Command suspended all RAF flights to Holland. (DVD Secret War - Episode 7 'The Dutch Disaster', Athena, 2011)

Foot reported Flying Officer Crow, of 138 Squadron, who had been shot down over Holland and testified that his air gunner had been shown a chart of his track, and that the Germans understood SOE's simple three torches signalling system used by the reception committees.

> *...the RAF had become worried at the rate of loss of extra precious aircrew, far more skilled than the bulk of Bomber Command at precise navigation, in special duty work over Holland. They lost twelve in the winter of 1942-3, one in every six sent: a loss rate of 18 per cent, far above the normal. In late May 1943 AI 2 (c), the corner of the Air Ministry than ran special operations, banned all such flights* (from Tempsford) *to the Netherlands for the time being. The ban was continued, from month to month, until the end of March 1944.* (Foot, op.cit. p. 175)

It was not until April 1944 that SOE was convinced that their Dutch circuits had been infiltrated and were being run by Germans. Given the secret nature of the organisations involved and the embarrassment to the British authorities, there have been conflicting reports. 138 Squadron records show that they lost eighty-three crew members on missions to Holland. Giskes' final sarcastic message to N Section on April Fools Day was transmitted simultaneously on ten captured wireless sets :

> For Messrs Blunt [Blizard's codename], Bingham and Successors Ltd We understand that you have been

Halifax DG245 of 138 Squadron, RAF Tempsford. A hole was cut in the bottom of the fuselage to allow containers and parachutists to be dropped into Belgium and other countries in occupied Europe.

(In Freddy Clark's *Agents by Moonlight* courtesy of P.R.O. Kew)

Westland Lysander used to take and pick up agents and VIPs from Tempsford (and RAF Tangmere on south coast). Note the ladder to allow quicker access.

(www.jaapteeuwen.com/.../westland%20lysander.jpg)

View approaching RAF Tempsford from the south.
October 13th 1942
(Courtesy of RAF Museum, Hendon)

Aerial photograph of RAF Tempsford 1943. It was designed by an illusionist to give the appearance that it was a disused airfield. Agents sent into Belgium and other destinations in occupied Europe were flown from here.
(Courtesy of Harrington Aviation Museum)

Gibraltar Farm, Tempsford Airfield, Bedfordshire, the nerve centre of SO TOP SECRET airfield. Hitler is said to have called it a viper's nest but it w never attacked throughout the war. Agents were given their final briefing the farmhouse.

http://www.wartimememories.co.uk/airfields/GibralterFarm-1.jpg 29 October 2009

The barn, all that remains of Gibraltar Farm. It was in here where Belgian and other agents were checked by an RAF officer to ensure they had no incriminating items on their person. They were kitted out with parachute, harness, helmet, gloves, ankle supports, boots, and a choice of dagger or revolver, a flask of whisky, rum or brandy and a choice of pills—one of which was cyanide.

(Courtesy of John Button)

Inside of the barn showing the concrete shelving on which parachutes, harnesses and other supplies for the agents were stored. It is now a memorial to the brave deeds of the men and women of every nationality who left for their missions from here.

(Courtesy of Bernard O'Connor)

The Control Tower or "Watchtower' of Tempsford Airfield. Its codename was BRASSTRAY.

(http://www.deborahjackson.net/assets/images/timemeddlers2_tempsford 29

> endeavouring for some time to do business in Netherlands without our assistance. We regret this the more since we have acted so long as your sole representatives in this country to our mutual satisfaction. Nevertheless we can assure you that if you are thinking of paying us a visit on the Continent on any extensive scale we shall give your emissaries the same attention as we have hitherto and a similarly warm welcome. Hoping to see you. (TNA HS 6/736 Hans Giskes, 1 April 1944)

Giskes was said to have controlled up to eighteen different radio channels and picked up, forty-six British agents including nine from MI6 and one from MI9 as well as fifty-one Dutch agents. Between 200 and 350 resistance members were arrested. Marks noted that, in November 1943, fifty-five imprisoned agents were shot on the orders of the Gestapo in an attempt to keep the Englandspiel a secret. (Marks, op.cit.)

Foot's research into the testimony of Joseph Schreieder, the *Kriminaldirektor* of SS *Sturmbannfuhrer* in Holland, stated that, between March 1941 and August 1943, *Englandspiel* had eighteen wireless lines to England under the control of German Military Counter Espionage officers. Through them they ordered 190 supply drops to fourteen locations in the Dutch heath lands and picked up 570 containers, about 150 parcels and arrested fifty-three agents. They got 15,200 kilograms of explosives, 3,000 Sten guns, 300 Bren guns, 5,000 pistols, 2,000 hand grenades, seventy-five wireless sets, 100 torchlights, six muffler pistols, three wireless direction finders (Eurekas), three walkie-talkies (S-Phones), two infra-red torch lights, more than 500,000 cartridges, 15,000 kilograms of explosives and more than

500,000 Guilden in Dutch currency. What was particularly worrying was that the missions continued for so long. (Foot, op.cit. p.189)

A report by Paul Lashmar and Chris Staerk in *The Independent* said that SOE files reveal that, up to October 1943, SOE had sent fifty-six agents to Holland of which forty-three were given a 'reception' by the Germans. Of the fifty-six, only eight survived. Of those captured, thirty-six were executed in September 1944 at Mauthausen concentration camp, about twenty kilometres east of Linz in Austria.

According to the 'Dutch Disaster' episode on the 'Secret War' DVD, from ninety RAF sorties the Germans captured fifty-eight agents and collected an estimated fifteen tons of weapons, 500,000 guilders, fifty-three wireless sets, 900 machine guns, 2,000 pistols and revolvers, 8,000 hand grenades and 15,000 rounds of ammunition. The researchers for the documentary claim that documents show that N section had been penetrated by 'a double-double agent' and referred to Dutch journalists identifying Bingham as he had been born in Holland and had a relative who worked for Giskes and Schreieder during the war. Many documents relating to the Englandspiel were burnt in a fire after the war and others have been closed by the National Archives until 2031. (DVD 'Secret War - Episode 7 The Dutch Disaster', Athena, 2011)

Exactly how many women were sent to other countries in occupied Europe is uncertain. My research so far has identified over sixty. *Return to Belgium* tells the story of three Belgian women who had got out of the country and volunteered to be trained by the SOE and parachuted back. Another who was understandably anonymous, was sent in by the SIS to engage in obtaining intelligence through 'horizontal collaboration'. The other three were dropped on consecutive nights in early August 1944 into Belgium and northern France. Their top secret missions were to assist the Allies in their invasion plans and included reporting on enemy troop movements, attempting to extricate a member of the Belgian royal family and promoting propaganda, prostitution, drugs and alcohol in an attempt to rot the German's morale. (O'Connor, B. *Return to Belgium,* www.lulu.com, 2012)

There are no records of any women being dropped into Denmark. There might have been one but the evidence is uncertain. In David Oliver's *Airborne Espionage* he quotes Roy Buckingham who was posted to 138 Squadron in June 1944.

> *On one occasion we had to bring our 'Joe', a young lady, back with us to the forward base at Kinloss in Scotland after the 'Joe' hatch had frozen solid over a DZ in Denmark.*
> *It was my duty with Bill Clarkson, the dispatcher, to make sure that no-one talked to the agent while we were away from the base. We had to stick close to her even in bed — we were all fully clothed - and when she went to the toilet, the door remained unlocked. We were standing outside the women's toilet when a senior WAAF officer wanted to go in. We barred her way and she demanded to speak to our commanding officer. We gave her the number and when she got through, her face went bright red when he told her in no uncertain terms that she should leave us to do our duty.* (Oliver, D. *Airborne Espionage,* The History Press, (2005)

Who she was, what her mission was and whether she went on a subsequent mission remains a mystery. I have found evidence of three women sent into Holland. Details of their missions are revealed in their personnel files in the National Archives in Kew. The first was 31-year-old Beatrice 'Trix' Terwindt, identified by MI9, the British government's secret organisation responsible for returning downed aircrew to England, as being the ideal person for running a new escape line.

As shall be seen, she had managed to get out of Belgium during the war and reached England in the late summer of 1942. All overseas immigrants during the war were interviewed in depth, many of them at the Royal Victorian Patriotic School in Wandsworth, south London. The people in British intelligence were keen to obtain up-to-date information about what life was really like in other parts of the world as well as to determine whether or not they were interviewing a German agent. The SIS was also keenly interested as it provided details of the escape lines that had been used. The names, addresses, prices and times that Trix provided were valuable intelligence.

In the report following her interview on 27 August, Trix's height was given as five feet eight inches. She had a high forehead, brown eyes, short, dark curly hair, was of a dark complexion and had a long high-bridged nose and round chin. According to her interviewer's report, she was born on 27 February 1911 and grew up in Arnhem, the seventh child of a Belgian noblewoman and a Dutch father. He used to run a stone quarry and worked as a pottery manufacturer until he retired. A supporter of the Roman Catholic Conservative Party, he had been a member of the *Nederlandsche Unie,* one of the Dutch political parties, until it was banned by the German authorities. (The

Audley End House, Essex, where, early in the war, some Dutch and other agents were accommodated before being driven to Newmarket racecourse for their flight into Europe.
(http://www.grouptravelorganiser.com/assets/8/7/Audleyend_fullsize.jpg 23 August 2009)

Chicheley Park, Newport Pagnell, Buckinghamshire, where, from 1940—1942, Dutch agents were housed before being sent on missions by the Special Duties Squadrons.

http://farm4.static.flickr.com/3070/2610352907_3866e226ca_o.jpg 27 October 2009

Gaynes Hall, Cambridgeshire, where, from 1942—1944 Dutch and other agents were accommodated prior to being driven to RAF Tempsford or RAF Harrington for their missions.
(http://upload.wikimedia.org/wikipedia/en/5/5f/Gaynes_Hall_tmb.jpg 23 August 2009)

Hasells Hall, Sandy. Officers Mess. Some agents stayed there before flights
(Stan Tomlinson)

National Archives (TNA) HS 9/452/8)

After attending elementary and high school in Arnhem, she spent six months at the English Convent School in Bruges and six months at the Convent Helmet in Brussels until she was seventeen. Fluent in English and Frenchm she also knew some German. After two years at the Arnhem School of Art, she studied modern interior decoration at the Amsterdam School of Art for a year. When she was twenty, she returned to Arnhem to study for a course at the Netherlands Art Institute in Rome. This fell though for financial reasons and the institute deciding to only take on Dutch citizens living in Italy. Instead she attended the Sittard Commercial College studying Librarianship. Failing the examination at the end of her second year, she got a job at the beginning of 1935 working at the *Stolz Kunstzaal de Gulden Roos*, an art gallery in Maastricht, giving advice on modern interior decoration and furnishings. From May 1936 until the end of the year she did a variety of jobs, mainly translating French books into Dutch, and living with the family of Anton Aerts, the director of the newspaper *Nieuwe Tilburgsche Courant*, at 52 Schouweg, Wassenaar, between the Hague and Lieden.

At the beginning of 1937 she was successful in getting a job as an air hostess for KLM, the Dutch airline company, employed on all their European routes. When war broke out nearly all KLM's flights were cancelled so, with no work to do, she was laid off but paid a retainer. After six months working at Bjenkorf, Amsterdam's largest department store and living on the Lange Leidschedwarstraat, she was taken on at Schifol airport doing secretarial work for KLM.

Following the German invasion on 10 March 1940 she was transferred to the Hague to work in the company's offices, initially to assist in fuel distribution but later to work in their Welfare and Advice bureau for evacuees from Rotterdam. This work lasted until the beginning of June 1941 when, still being paid a retaining fee, she went to live in the Cuddelstraat in Aalsmeer to act as a link between Klaas Voute, the Brussels representative of KLM and the farmers in the rural areas around Utrecht.

Voute wanted her to help them arrange safe houses, food and medicine for shot down RAF pilots and their onward escape out of Holland, through Belgium and France and freedom via the neutral countries of Switzerland, Spain or Portugal. He had been the secretary of the *Nederlandsche Unie,* of which her father had been a member, and she was convinced that he was in touch with the British Secret Service. Whilst there, she helped him by distributing copies of *Vrij Nederland,* a left-wing underground newspaper started after German occupation. She told her interviewer that he had been arrested and imprisoned.

As she had been unemployed for five months, she avoided having to register with the Dutch Labour Exchange by going back in November 1941 to work for KLM as a secretary for Dr. Foucher, who worked in the Flying Service. There was very little for her to do. Whilst in Amsterdam, the navigation instructor at KLM, a Mr. Kellenbach who lived in Scheldeplein, introduced her to Theo Lusinck, one of his cadets. She agreed to escort Lusinck to Switzerland and learned that Kellenbach was involved in the Melser organisation, an escape line based in The Hague, which helped get downed RAF pilots, crews and other evaders out of Holland. Lusinck was keen to get out as his parents, true Oranje patriots, were putting pressure on him, arguing that he would do his country a far better service by leaving it and joining the Dutch Free

Clip of the barn where Trix Terwindt was taken by the German reception committee.

(Clip from the History Channel's 'The Spying Game', 2007)

Clip of the secluded villa where Trix Terwindt was taken for her first interrogation by the Gestapo.

(Clip from the History Channel's 'The Spying Game', 2007)

Forces in England. Trix must have shown some sympathy for him as Kellenback asked her to accompany him as he knew she was also keen to escape and do something more useful.

Things came to a head on or about 14 March 1942 following the arrest of Dr. Foucher. Whether he was also involved in the Melser organisation is unknown. Voute and Kellenbach gave them instructions, addresses and presumably money as on 20 March she caught a train to Tilburg with Lusinck and then walked to the house of their first contact, a Mr Van der Pol, an ex-Customs official who lived in a nearby village. At about 1500 hours he took them across the border into Belgium where they were able to change money at a local farm. The farmer's daughter took them down the road and showed them how to get to Turnhout, about 12 miles (20 kms) to the south. From there they caught the train to Antwerp, changed for Brussels and spent the night at a café close to the station run by a Mlle. Rosa.

The next morning, 21 March, they caught the train to Heeragimont where they contacted the Roman Catholic priest. He told them how to get to Civet over the *Petit Chemin* without meeting any controls. They spent the night there at the café Rexi. The following day they caught the train to Nancy, spent the night in the waiting room and caught the morning train to Epinal. There they spent the night in a small hotel near the station and continued by train to Besancon, via Vesoul on 24 March.

The next safe house, the café du Theatre, proved difficult to find but the people she talked to appeared to know nothing of an evasion route but did suggest that, if they took the bus to Arbois, they might be able to find a *passeur*, a guide, who would take them across the border into Switzerland. Unaware of the controls, they caught a bus at 1600 hours and arrived just after dark. With a stroke of luck they followed a German officer off the bus who, being of some importance, was engaged in conversation with the guard checking passengers, which allowed them to slip away unnoticed.

When she contacted the Roman Catholic priest in Arbois, he seemed afraid to help but suggested they might find a place for the night at the Red Cross post. Luckily, a woman who they asked for directions, took them to a small hotel where they were given a room. The proprietress told them that they were fortunate as there was a French *passeur* staying there that night who helped French escaped prisoners cross the border. He was introduced to them as Marcel Thiebaud.

The next day, 26 March, at 1230 hours he took them, another woman and four French escapees straight through the woods and, without keeping to any particular path, managed to get them to Poligne, where they arrived between 2000 and 2030 hours. He somehow found a car and drove them to St. Julien, where they all spent the evening in the hotel and the following day, at about 1130 hours he dropped them at Collonges, where the road runs along the Swiss border and left them to cross by themselves.

They went into a café but the woman who worked there did not think they could cross there. However, one of the other customers told them that he would help. But, at the point where he suggested they could get across, they saw the Frontier Police so decided to return to the café.

Whilst deliberating as to what to do next, a French Customs official entered the café and sat down for a meal. In a subsequent conversation he guessed their intent and told them that he was going back on duty at 1500 hours and could assist them by not seeing them. He even indicated the best

Antonia Hamilton

Born in Breda in 1910 she accompanied her parents to New York in 1932. returned to Amsterdam in 1938. Came to Britain, trained by SOE, parachuted near Abberkerk on 10 August 1944 and broke her leg which required hospital treatment and long term care.

(National Archives HS 6/767)

Frank Hamilton

Dropped with his sister Antonia on 10 August 1944. Code-named Guus, known in the field as Frans Hertog.

(National Archives HS 6/767)

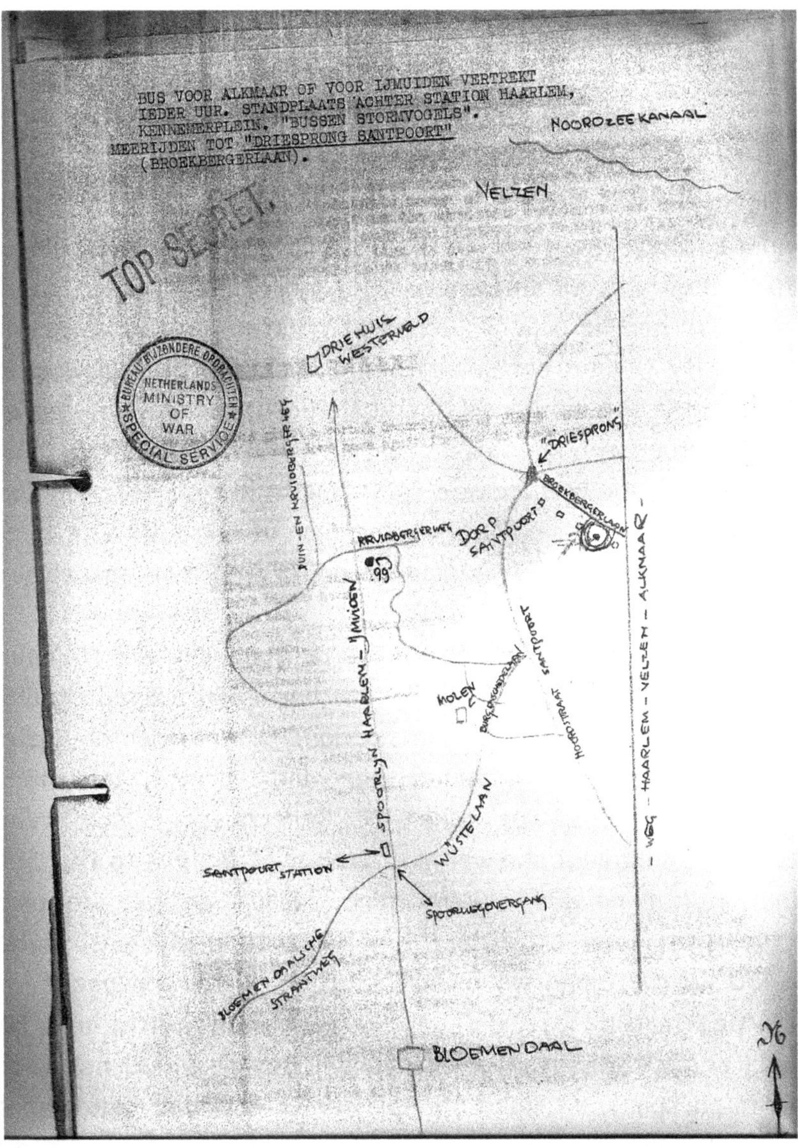

BUS VOOR ALKMAAR OF VOOR IJMUIDEN VERTREKT
IEDER UUR. STANDPLAATS ACHTER STATION HAARLEM,
KENNEMERPLEIN. "BUSSEN STORMVOGELS".
MEERIJDEN TOT "DRIESPRONG SANTPOORT"
(BROEKBERGERLAAN).

Plan attached to the Hamiltons personal file showing the location of their first contact, Guardmaster de Vries in Santpoort.
(National Archives HS 6/767)

place to cross, which path to take round the corner of the field.

Trix and Lusinck set off and ran at top speed for about 200 metres over the border until they ran into a Swiss border official, He took them to his post and rang the Military Police in Geneva. They then had to wait for him to arrive in his car. When they got out in Geneva they were interrogated and, as they both had no papers, were not trusted until Trix was able to identify from a list shown her a Miss Van Zanten, someone whose name she may have been given as a contact by Voute or Kellenbach or who she knew from her work with KLM. Following a phone call, she was allowed to stay with her at Hotel du Lac in Vesenaz. There was no further mention of Lusinck. Whether he managed to get to England is unknown. Trix had to carry on, apparently alone.

Three weeks later, on Saturday 18 April, she was taken into what she called "quarantine". A law had been passed requiring anyone who had arrived in Switzerland after a certain date in March - and that included her and Lusinck, had to be incarcerated. She was taken to Bellechasse Prison. Whilst inside she said that she wrote a number of letters to the Dutch legation but none of them were passed on by the prison authorities. However, without any explanation, she was released on 30 April, along with some other Dutch refugees, and returned to the Hotel du Lac. The room was said to have been paid for by the Dutch government. They provided her with a Dutch passport, stamped 15 April 1942, and told her that she had been allowed to go to England but she needed to obtain a visa for Curaçao in the Dutch Antilles and another for Brazil. Presumably, the plan was for her to board a ship bound for South America but to disembark in Lisbon or Gibraltar.

When these had been obtained for her, General Van Trio, the Military Attaché at the Dutch Legation in Berne, wrote her a 'Letter of Introduction to Diplomatic and Consular Officials Abroad'. Armed with these, she left Switzerland on the 2 July 1942 in what she called the "sealed" train with the Dutch convoy for Barcelona. It went via Cerbere and Port Bou.

From Barcelona she was sent on the 5 July to Bilbao on the north coast of Spain from where she was to take the SS *Cabo de Hornas* which was to leave on the 28. In the meantime, she stayed at the Hotel Excelsior and later at the Grand Pension Imperial. Whilst there she obtained her British visa but the Portuguese authorities refused her a visa against the one she had for Curaçao. When she learned that there was no chance of the British authorities allowing her to disembark at Gibraltar, she decided not to take the boat and, instead, used her British visa to claim a Portuguese visa.

The embassy in Lisbon was telegraphed and she was promised she would get it. As the ship had left, she had to make her way to Cadiz to catch it and she arrived there on 1 August 1942 and stayed in the Hotel Francienne y Paris. A fortnight later the visa had still not arrived. She was told that the Bilbao office hadn't sent the confirmation to Cadiz. Forgetting the boat option she caught the train to Madrid on the 15 August where, on the 19, the Portuguese Consulate granted her the visa without further ado. Whilst in the Spanish capital she stayed at the Hotel Mora and, with the help of the Dutch legation, managed to get the exit visa needed to leave the country and an airline ticket for Lisbon.

On 23 August she arrived in the Portuguese capital and stayed at the Grand Hotel Estoril, courtesy of KLM and, two days later caught the aircraft G-AGBB to England. She arrived at Whitchurch airport on the 26 August and was taken to be debriefed, like all immigrants into the country, at the Royal British Patriotic School. The report, signed R. S.

Sands, concluded:

> *Miss TERWINDT - although unable to remember a number of names - gave her account in a convincing and straightforward manner. She is well-educated and comes of a good Dutch family. Whilst with the K.L.M. she had 3,000 flying hours to her credit. From cross-examination I have come to the conclusion that she is a plucky and sensible little patriot and I have not the slightest reason to believe that she offers any security interest. She does not want to take up an administrative job here for the Dutch Government - all she is interested in, and for which purpose she has made her way to this country, is active participation in the war effort either for the K.L.M. or some other war work.*
>
> *RECOMMENDATION.*
>
> *I have no hesitation at all in recommending her early release to the Dutch Authorities.* (TNA HS 9/1452/8)

After her interrogation, Trix was provided with accommodation in a house on Nightingale Lane in Wandsworth. With an interest in 'active participation in the war effort', she was prime material for Special Operations. It was only a matter of weeks therefore before she was identified by the SIS as a valuable contact for M.I. 9, the Foreign Office's agency for covert operations. Dr. R. P. Derksema, who had taken over from 't Sant as head of Dutch intelligence in London, recommended her to Airey Neave who had recently returned to England himself after successfully escaping from German imprisonment at Colditz Castle. Readers may know of him after the war as being a Conservative MP and being

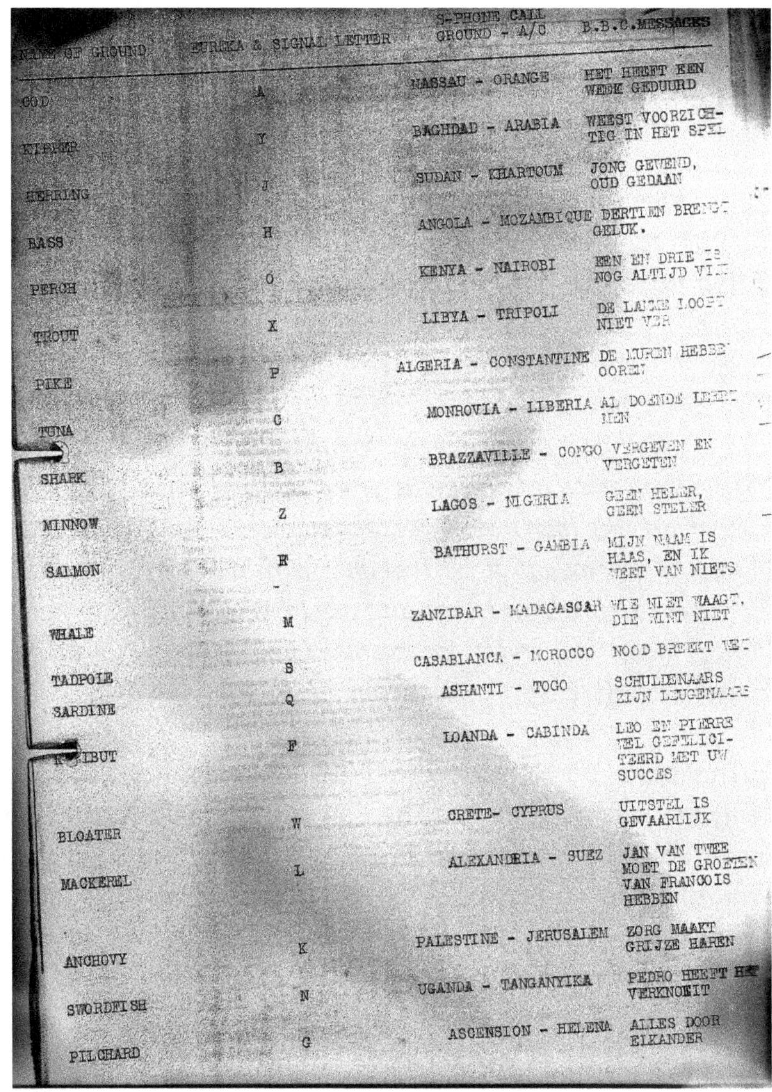

NAME OF GROUND	EUREKA & SIGNAL LETTER	S-PHONE CALL GROUND - A/C	B.B.C. MESSAGES
COD	A	NASSAU - ORANGE	HET HEEFT EEN WEEK GEDUURD
KIPPER	Y	BAGHDAD - ARABIA	WEEST VOORZICH-TIG IN HET SPEL
HERRING	J	SUDAN - KHARTOUM	JONG GEWEND, OUD GEDAAN
BASS	H	ANGOLA - MOZAMBIQUE	DERTIEN BRENGT GELUK.
PERCH	O	KENYA - NAIROBI	EEN EN DRIE IS NOG ALTIJD VIER
TROUT	X	LIBYA - TRIPOLI	DE LANGE LOOPT NIET VER
PIKE	P	ALGERIA - CONSTANTINE	DE MUREN HEBBEN OOREN
TUNA	C	MONROVIA - LIBERIA	AL DOENDE LEERT MEN
SHARK	B	BRAZZAVILLE - CONGO	VERGEVEN EN VERGETEN
MINNOW	Z	LAGOS - NIGERIA	GEEN HELER, GEEN STELER
SALMON	R	BATHURST - GAMBIA	MIJN NAAM IS HAAS, EN IK WEET VAN NIETS
WHALE	M	ZANZIBAR - MADAGASCAR	WIE NIET WAAGT, DIE WINT NIET
TADPOLE	S	CASABLANCA - MOROCCO	NOOD BREEKT WET
SARDINE	Q	ASHANTI - TOGO	SCHULDENAARS ZIJN LEUGENAARS
K[illegible]IBUT	F	LOANDA - CABINDA	LEO EN PIERRE WEL GEFELICI-TEERD MET UW SUCCES
BLOATER	W	CRETE- CYPRUS	UITSTEL IS GEVAARLIJK
MACKEREL	L	ALEXANDRIA - SUEZ	JAN VAN TWEE MOET DE GROETEN VAN FRANCOIS HEBBEN
ANCHOVY	K	PALESTINE - JERUSALEM	ZORG MAAKT GRIJZE HAREN
SWORDFISH	N	UGANDA - TANGANYIKA	PEDRO HEEFT HET VERKNOEIT
PILCHARD	G	ASCENSION - HELENA	ALLES DOOR ELKANDER

Copy of the microfilm giving the code names of 20 drop zones, the signal letter for the Eureka direction finding beacon, the S-Phone (ground to air radio communication) codenames as well as the BBC messages that indicated the mission was on.

(TNA HS 6/767)

assassinated by the I.R.A. in a car bomb in Ireland. When he met Trix he described her as

> "*slim and dark with intelligent grey eyes. In out first conversation, I found her quiet and thoughtful and eager to return to Holland. I had no doubt that she possessed both courage and resolution, qualities which she was later to demonstrate in awful circumstances.*
>
> *...She had a strong personality, but she would not easily be noticed on trains or at control points and she seemed like many of the girls employed by Comet She was efficient and practical and, with a supply of Dutch money, I concluded that she would be able to help with the many domestic problems involved in sheltering airmen."* (Neave, A. *Saturday at MI9*)

There was no mention in her personal file how to where the money had come from. The Comet or Comète escape line was established Brussels in 1940 to get Belgian soldiers and down Allied air crews out of Belgium. Its two early founders had been captured so it was Andrée de Jong, a young Belgian woman, who took over the reins and helped get evaders through France and into Spain. Once there, they could make their way to Lisbon or Gibraltar and back to Britain.

In Neave's *Saturday at M.I.9* he tells how the Comète line worked alongside the PAT escape line which had been established by Ian Garrow, a soldier in the British Expeditionary Forces who had missed the Dunkirk evacuation and remained in France. When he was arrested in October 1941 the network was taken over by Albert

Guérisse, a Belgian military doctor, known by the alias Pat O'Leary. He had managed to get back to England, was trained by the SOE and sent back to help get evaders out. Although initially based near Perpignan, his network had safe houses in Paris, Marseilles and Toulouse. The PAT line got evaders out from southeast France, either by boat from the Mediterranean coast, or over the eastern Pyrenees into Spain. The Comète line got people over the south-western Pyrenees to the British Consul in Bilbao.

The Nazis' successful penetration of both lines led to numerous arrests which were threatening their continuation. Despite Andrée's father and elder sister being among them, she continued until the Gestapo caught her in August 1942. The line was continued, headed by Baron Jean Greindl, but it worked with much tighter security. Micheline de Jongh, Andrée's younger sister, stepped in to do the courier work.

When O'Leary was arrested in March 1943, Mary Louise Dissard, like, took over the reins and continued the operation. She was a 62-year-old member of the resistance from Toulouse who the Germans never suspected as being involved until one of the evaders was captured along with a notebook containing her name and address. Forced to go into hiding, she lived in attics, cellars and garages until Toulouse was liberated on August 15 1944. The story can be found in *Return to Belgium.*

MI9 was keen to rebuild a secure network, with a link from Holland to Brussels, so that downed aircrews would have a chance to fight another day. As it cost £10,000 to train an RAF pilot, Britain wanted their money's worth out of them.

Neave's plan needed liaison with the SOE and the Special Duties Squadrons based at RAF Tempsford. Correspondence in her personal file shows how Neave tried to resolve the delicate matter with his SOE counterpart.

28 September 1942
Dear Major Blizard,

The subject of our recent conversation is a Dutchwoman, Miss Beatrice Terwindt (known as "TRIX"), who recently arrived in this country from Holland.

I was offered this lady's services by Captain Dirksmeer, and decided to employ her as she seemed willing to help organise the evacuation of R.A.F. from Holland, and had previously been in contact with an organisation there.

In order to send her back to Holland, I asked you for your help in arranging her reception there by boat or parachute, of which two methods I understand that the latter will be the easiest for you. I gather that you are willing to do this, provided that you can reveal her employment by me to the Dutch, with whom you are working. I, myself, am quite prepared for you to do this, and I quite understand your reasons for wishing to do so. I am willing to take the risk of any repercussions among the rival factions which might result in making Miss Terwindt's employment by me a matter of difficulty. I should be glad, however, if you would let me know what, in any, objections your friends may raise, and I will try and straighten things out. Colonel Crockatt of M.I. 9. approves, and I am very grateful for your offer of help in this matter. I shall hope to hear from you in due course.

Yours sincerely,
Airey Neave . (TNA HS 9/1452/8)

One of Neave's colleagues wrote a note to Colonel

Norman Crockatt, head of M.I. 9, at Room 731, Metropole Buildings, W.C.2 dated 27 November 1943.

M.O.I. (S.P.)
My Dear Norman

I understand that Blizard, of this Department, has had some talk with Neave as to the suggestion that we might help you in connection with the mission of Beatrice TERWINDT.

I understand that her proposed mission is cleared with S.I.S. and accordingly, that any ordinary Security enquiries which could take place prior to our accepting her for training are dispensed with.

We shall be glad to arrange for training her in jumping, and if you wish it, and if time allows, we should try to arrange to have her sent to one of our Finishing Schools, particularly with a view to giving her some Security training in such matters as settling in in her territory of operations, making contacts, etc.

In view of the importance of her mission and our desire to cooperate with you in any way possible, I should be grateful if you would let me know in reply whether the above is in accordance with your wishes or whether there is anything else that we could usefully do.

Yours ever.

2 December
To: D/:M From: AD/F
Beatrice TERWINDT

I understand from Crockatt of M.I.9 that he passed to you my letter to him of 27 November as to

> *the training and mission of Beatrice TERWINDT since he points out that the operations of Langley and Neave are carried out under your instructions.* (Ibid.)

James Langley was a handsome young Guards officer who had lost an arm at Dunkirk and been taken prisoner. After escaping from a German military hospital at Lille, he made his way across France under his own initiative, and, after reaching Marseilles, managed to get in contact with the PAT escape line. When he got back to Britain in 1941 he got work with Airey Neave at MI9, They needed agents back in the field who could use a radio to receive and transmit messages, carry important messages and documents, distribute money and coordinate parachute drops.

Trix was one of over sixty women agents trained by the SOE for this kind of work. She started her initial 'Assessment Course' on the 1 December 1942 at Winterfold, using the cover name Miss Beatrice Thompson. After a fortnight of physical fitness training, map reading, orienteering, field craft, weapons and explosives training and psychological tests, she was sent for parachute training at Ringway airfield where agents underwent further fitness training, learning to land properly and how to jump from an air balloon and a plane. A note in her file dated 23 December 1942 stated that "*This student is being specially trained by us for despatch to the field, on behalf of M.I. 9, as a liaison officer. She has been at STS 5 and is now at STS 51.*"

Returning to London for Christmas, she spent New Year at S.T.S. 31. This was 'The Rings', one of the large country houses in the grounds of Beaulieu Abbey. Yet more fitness training, field craft, aircraft recognition, Morse code and other cipher training, burglary, safe breaking, sabotage, reception committee training, spy craft and even mock Gestapo interrogations was given. Part of the training included what was called a 'scheme', several days in an unknown town or city, practicing 'tailing' people, avoiding being followed herself, rendezvousing with contacts, identifying potential safe house and dead letter boxes.

She returned to London on 24 January 1943, the same day her report from her Finishing School was written, which read:

> *Miss Thompson*
>
> *She is very intelligent, capable, resourceful, practical and most discreet. She is hard-working, serious-minded and once she has grasped a point is quick to realise its application. She has had much experience of the world and has mixed freely with all types and classes of people. It would be very difficult indeed to deceive or impose on her.*
>
> *She has a very pleasant personality, quiet but forceful. At first sight both her appearance and manner are misleading; she seems shy, negative and almost "mousey" - actually she is quite the reverse. The deceptiveness of her appearance may be most helpful as she might easily go unnoticed. She should prove very clever at persuading others, particularly men, to help her on account of her apparent feminine weakness; she will easily win their confidence and trust.*
>
> *Her main difficulty is her innate lack of self-confidence, which she always overcomes but not without effort; this will subject her to constant nervous strain which may prove exhausting.*
>
> *As a leader she would be handicapped initially by her sex and manner, but once she has overcome these*

difficulties she should be a great success.

Codes report. Innocent letter (Playfair/Rimmer). Conventions fixed. She is at present proficient, but if she happens to remain for any length of time in this country she should have some regular practice. Simple inks. She has only elementary knowledge of this subject, but it should be adequate for her requirements. (Ibid.)

A week later she went back to Ringway for yet more parachute training. Perhaps the weather had been bad on her first visit. On 18 January, before the second part of her training at Beaulieu, the SOE received a note from the Belgian and Dutch Employment Exchange at Rutland Lodge, Rutland Gardens in Knightsbridge enquiring about Trix's status. Their response was that she was "now a student of this Section and in training." On 5 February 1943 Major O'Reilly at the War Office in Whitehall, knowing the plans for Trix's imminent departure, wrote to J. P. Balsdon at the Ministry of Labour and National Service at 15 Portman Square, London, W.1.

Dear Balsdon,
Beatrix TERWINDT
Would you please be so good as to pilot the attached document safely through your department?
Miss B. TERWINDT is, for your information, with this organisation. I would rather not say any more on paper as to her immediate future.
Perhaps you could instruct your Belgian/Dutch Section to Lay-off or mark up "otherwise employed".
Would you please confirm to me such official action you may take so that our papers can be marked appropriately? (Ibid.)

On the day she flew out from Tempsford a note in her file

acknowledged "*that the necessary steps had been taken to ensure that no further enquiries are to be made in the case of Miss Beatrice Terwindt.*" Everything was in place ready for what the SOE had called Operation CHICORY. Trix's codename was *Felix*. It was just a matter of waiting for an available plane when the weather was clear between the waxing and the waning of the moon.

An insight into what she must have gone through whilst she was waiting was provided in the personal file of Anne-Marie Walters, one of the women agents sent into France. When she returned to England after the war she was interviewed by a reporter working for the BBC radio. It was following a government announcement about women being sent as spies into France. Whether it was forced by the media suddenly discovering that women had been sent into occupied Europe as secret agents, one does not know but both the *Daily Express* and *Daily Telegraph* ran articles on female spies. What follows is the transcript of the interview in March 1945 that had to be sent to SOE for vetting. The text in bold was told to be deleted before the programme was allowed to transmit it.

CUE MATERIAL FOR PARACHUTE GIRL

On March 5, Sir Archibald Sinclair revealed for the first time in his speech to the Commons that members of the Women's Auxiliary Air Force have been to the fore in helping the Resistance groups in Europe before the landing on D-Day, either as Liaison officers, or couriers or radio operators.
We have in the studio today a girl who was parachuted into France many months before D-Day (and) *remained several months after fighting with the Maquis. This*

WAAF had an English father and a French mother and was brought up in Geneva and she begins this interview with Vera Lindsay by telling how she was chosen for this special work.

LINDSAY: Tell me - how was it you were chosen to be parachuted into France to do this special work?
PARA.GIRL: Well you see I was born and brought up in Geneva and my mother is French, so that I actually speak French much better than English. And what is more, consider that France is my country really from a patriotic point of view.
LINDSAY: Tell me - you came to England when, exactly?
PARA.GIRL: I came in 1940 just after the S.... had happened and I had actually never come to England before that.
LINDSAY: And what did you start doing? How did they find you?
PARA.GIRL: Well I was in the WAAFs and as I'd always made quite a lot of noise about being able to speak French and wanted to do some work having to do with the Free French and I had been on the list for transfer of jobs for some time.
LINDSAY: Tell me - how long did you train for this special work and was the training very difficult?
PARA.GIRL: Well I trained quite a long time, and the training was extremely interesting and very useful to me but I'm afraid I cannot talk at all about that right now.
LINDSAY: Were there other women training with you?
PARA.GIRL: Yes, there were a number of other women training with me. Quite a number trained after I left and

went later too,
LINDSAY: But were they English girls who spoke French?
PARA.GIRL: Some were French but most of them were English girls speaking absolutely fluent French. Actually French like a native woman.
LINDSAY: Now tell me, I know I can't ask you questions but tell me this - what is it like just before when you know already that you were - you had finished your training and were leaving for France? What were the days like just before that?
PARA.GIRL: Well to be quite honest they were rather nerve-racking, because we were supposed to leave in November 1943 but the weather was so bad, flying conditions were so poor that there was no question of leaving until the beginning of January. Every morning we'd call at our office at eleven o'clock and they invariably answered that the weather was too bad for that same night, but that we had to go on standing by and we just studied maps and studied the conditions of life in the particular region we were going to, and tried to get as much information as we could from this end of the work.
LINDSAY: But what about the region you were going to? Did you know it at all?
PARA.GIRL: No, I didn't know it at all and as a matter of fact it was particularly chosen so that I shouldn't. So that I should not run the risk of falling into people who had seen me going and leaving France and who knew that I hadn't been in France the last years and who obviously would immediately guess how I had arrived and what I was doing.
LINDSAY: But in those days just before you left were you able to see ordinary people? I mean your friends in

London?

PARA.GIRL: Well the only people I knew and frequented so to speak were my friends who were doing the same job as I was and my family didn't know anything about it and we had worked out all our stories to the last details. Whenever they came at home they never mentioned anything of the work we were doing. My parents knew I was doing secret work but they didn't know at all, they didn't have any idea what it was. And my friends played up to the game very well.

LINDSAY: And tell me, how are you dressed for this, for this dropping from the sky into France?

PARA.GIRL: I was dressed exactly as I am now walking around in the streets of London. I had a tweed suit on and a fur coat and I had some a jump suit on top of course - but the idea was that I should be just one of the crowd of people in France as soon as I arrived there.

LINDSAY: And just before the jump - what was the feeling? Were you afraid?

PARA.GIRL: No, I wasn't afraid. In fact it was the only time in all the jumps that I have made that I really wasn't afraid at all. There were so many things to think about and it was our second trip. The pilot had circled some time in the region before being able to contact our people on the ground and we had a horrible moment that we should have to go back once more. And when the pilot declared that he had contacted the people and we were to go to action stations and jump - I felt so relieved at the idea that we wouldn't have to go back again to England it was really quite a pleasure.

LINDSAY: And tell me - did you feel very much in danger from the moment you landed?

PARA.GIRL: Well at first I did - I felt very obvious

- I had a feeling that I was so obvious as I would have been if I had been walking on the maps that I had been studying all that time just before leaving - but that's a feeling that soon left me and I was very easily - very easy to disappear in the crowd.
LINDSAY: Where did you live during the time that you were there?
PARA.GIRL: I lived in a farm the whole time. The farmers acted like parents to me. They never even asked me for a single centime in repayment for all they were doing for me. And they looked after me and helped me and the whole time and they weren't even worried about me - about themselves actually.
LINDSAY: Did they know what you were doing?
PARA.GIRL: Yes they did - of course it's too much to ask of anybody to be doing a thing like that without knowing what dangers they were risking.
LINDSAY: Yes but how did they - what did they say to the neighbours - I means how did they explain your arrival?
PARA.GIRL: Well everybody said that I was a student from Paris who just couldn't go on with her studies because life in Paris was so expensive and so different and who had come to seek refuge with the farmer who was supposed to be a friend of my father in the last war. That story took very well. It was very simple and normal there and everybody around the farm believed it and I should think they still believe it to this day. (TNA HS 9/229/2)

Because of the Atlantik Wall, the heavily defended coastal defences, radar stations, night-fighter bases and heavy and light anti-aircraft guns facing west towards

England, the 138 pilots approach to Holland was from the north over the Afsluitdijk and Zuyder Zee. The reception committee was using the standard lights procedure to guide the pilot to the drop zone. In typed instructions issued to the agents responsible for drops it advised that:

> *Air operations have often failed owing to lack of adequate ground lights. These lights must be as strong as possible and clearly visible up to a height of 600 metres. They should have an arc of 60°.*
>
> *The dropping area should be marked by two red torches and one white arranged as follows:*

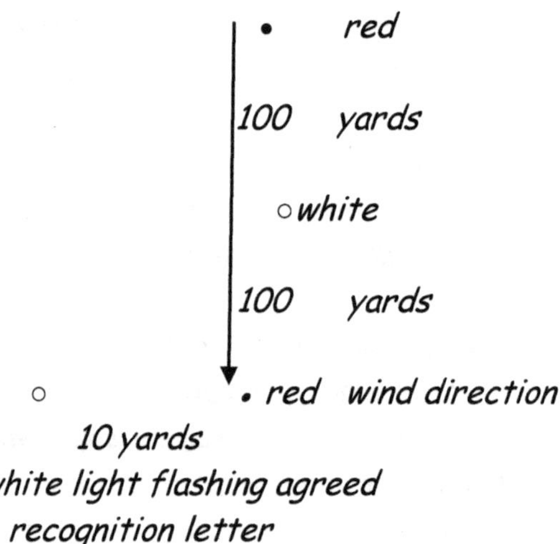

> *One additional white torch (flashing the agreed recognition letter) should be placed at the downwind end of the line so as to indicate to the aircraft the direction of the wind.*
>
> *On hearing the approaching aircraft, the lights should be switched on and your recognition letter should be flashed continuously until you see the aircraft has*

started to drop its load. The torches should be held at arm's length and pointed towards the aircraft throughout the operation until it has been completed. It is essential that the pilot should be able to see the lights the whole time, especially when he has once been over and is circling in order to make his run-up.

On seeing the lighting system, the aircraft will approach flying upwind and will release the load when approximately over the last red torch. The wind will cause the load to drift back to the field.

Before extinguishing your lights make sure you have your complete load as, if the aircraft is carrying a large load it may make two run-ups. (TNA HS 6/767)

In his autobiography, *Saturday at* M19, Neave expressed concerns that Trix might have been recognised by her KLM and other friends. Although he acknowledged that she might be able to explain away her absence as hiding from the Germans, he

...considered whether her appearance should not in some way be altered. Plastic surgery of the face to alter distinctive features was used on rare occasions during the Second World War, but this drastic method seemed unjustified. I took her to a sumptuous apartment at Albany in Piccadilly where we interviewed an expert in theatrical make-up who had nothing more original to suggest than altering her shoulders and hipline, by padding out her coat and skirt. (Neave, op.cit)

Neave must have discussed with her the contacts that she had had with Voute, Kellenbach and Foucher and felt she was in a position to establish useful links to strengthen the escape line. However, he warned her about two collaborators, Poos and Slagter, Dutch policemen working for the Germans. Where he got this information which ought to have been passed to the SOE, was not mentioned. Whether she was given detailed descriptions of them, given what subsequently happened, seems doubtful. What was also kept from her was news that he had received from Spain that Peggy van Leir and Count Edouard d'Oultremont, two important guides in the Comète line, had just escaped over the Pyrenees with news of arrests. It would be futile for Trix to try and rendezvous with any of the resistance in those conditions. The flight was therefore delayed until the following moon.

> *This meant a dismal period of waiting in London for her. The secrecy which we imposed on agents was depressing for this conscientious girl. She had now left the Training School and was obliged to remain alone in a dreary bed-sitting room in Kensington. I could understand her feelings but she realised the tremendous risks of associating with other Dutch agents. That she knew so little about S.O.E. and its organisation might well have saved her life.* (Ibid.)

On the evening of 13th February 1943, Neave escorted her by car to Tempsford airfield. After a final briefing over the map table in Gibraltar Farm, she was taken to the barn. After all the checks and being kitted out, he helped her into her parachute harness, handed her some Dutch guilders and forged identity papers as a hospital nurse named Johanna Maria van der Velden.

That morning he had received a telegram telling him that Baron Jean Greindl had been arrested. Known as Nemo, when

Peggy and Edouard escaped, he had agreed to stay behind and continue the running of the Comète line in Brussels. Neave didn't tell Trix but warned her not to make any attempt to contact the Comète line. Instead she had to spend the next few weeks finding safe houses and recruiting helpers. When she landed she was told to follow the reception committee's instructions for the first twenty -four hours and then make her own way to the Bally shoe shop in The Hague and contact a Monsieur Smit.

Having overcome her fear of parachuting, Trix was the first woman agent to be dropped into Holland, along with several containers, one of which included her wireless set. Unbeknownst to her or the pilot, the Germans had arranged everything. In Michael Foot's *SOE in the Low Countries,* he stated that N Section had been notorious for its severe rate of loss. Of the 137 agents sent in, sixty-six failed to return. Many had been captured almost as soon as they landed, taken away to be interrogated and tortured to get information out of them.

Once was safely on board, 138 Squadron's Operations Record Book shows that Squadron Leader Gibson took off carrying six containers, four packages, four boxes of chocolate and CHICORY 9, the name used for Trix's drop. Unfortunately, the EBENEEZER reception committee was not what she was expecting.

Trix jarred herself badly and hurt her face when the wind caught her parachute as she was landing in fields near Kallenkote, just outside Steenwijk, a small farming community about twelve miles (20 kms.) southwest of Groningen. Whilst some in the welcome committee collected the containers, unbeknown to her, Poos and Slagter helped disentangle her from her chute and harness. She thought they were a rough bunch of men but didn't think that their conversation was unusual for agents in the field. They sounded very convincing, asking her for her code, hidden in her cigarette lighter. When she replied that her orders were to divulge it to no-one, they complained that communications with London were bad and that they didn't understand their problems. Nor did they realise how dangerous conditions in Holland had become.

As they were walking across the field to the road she was told that the chief of the organisation would not be pleased to have a woman working for the Dutch underground. It was too rough. Whilst it annoyed her, it did not make her suspicious. The collaborators checked her identity papers and suggested that they had been badly printed in London and too dangerous to travel with. They recommended that she should wait until they could supply her with new ones. As she had to rendezvous with Smit, they managed to coax his address from her. According to Foot, they explained that London was often out of date with its addresses and they could not take responsibility for letting her continue with her mission until they had checked it out for her. Believing them to be genuine Dutch resistance members, she gave them Smit's address.

As it was raining, they sheltered her in a nearby wooden barn. Suddenly, someone threw a grey blanket over her head. They told her that her light raincoat was too conspicuous to be wearing in the dark. Thinking she was having her nerves tested like when she was rudely awoken at Beaulieu and subjected to brutal Gestapo interrogation 'practices', she didn't resist as forcefully as she'd been trained. When she felt being pushed lightly in the back, she put her hand behind her to find out what it was. Both arms were grabbed from behind and her wrists handcuffed before she could manage to get her poison pill into her mouth.

Taken to a secluded villa in the nearby countryside, she was interrogated for three days and nights. She claimed that they knew everything about the agents' training courses, where the grandfather clocks were and what tiles there were on the floor. The Abwehr were enjoying themselves.

Trix reported after the war that she was surprised at how much more her captors knew about the SOE than she did and was perturbed that the Germans couldn't understand why the British had sent a lone girl who evidently was very poorly briefed about her organisation. Apparently, they didn't realise she was from another covert operations department.

Afterwards she was then taken to Haaren, a requisitioned Catholic seminary, between Tilburg and s'Hertenbosch, used by the SD as a prison. Here she found herself amongst the other captured SOE agents. Kept in a cell all to herself whilst others were in twos or threes, she was left to worry about what might happen to her and what might happen to Smit.

Foot commented on how much information the interrogators had managed to extract from captured agents. *Sturmbannfuhrer* Joseph Schreieder, the head of counter-espionage and counter-sabotage in Holland, supervised the questioning. Trix said that he promised her that she wouldn't be sent to a concentration camp if she cooperated with him. What she did tell him is unknown but Neave asserts that she did not give him her wireless code.

His friendly manner then changed. He told Trix that he had means of making her talk but, she said that he didn't employ them. She thought he was the cleverest and most 'professional' of all the *Sicherheitsdienst* officers in charge of State Security.

In the Appendix of his *SOE in the Low* Countries Foot included a list of one hundred questions Schreieder wanted captured agents to be asked. A copy can be found at the back of this book which makes fascinating reading. Foot mentioned that

> *The prisoners who talked produced a cumulative impact: the pile of data in German hands got bigger and bigger, with less and less happy results for later victims. When the interrogator could describe the colour of the wallpaper in a Beaulieu classroom, and distinguish which of the staff wore glasses, and which wore moustaches, which smoked cigarettes and which preferred a pipe, it was not easy for a newcomer to resist the belief that All was Known. No one seems to have succeeded with the simple counter, 'If you know so much, why bother me?'*
>
> *Only those who have crossed that grim strait could ever describe - none, I believe, has - what it feels like to pass suddenly from believing one is 'un dur des durs' to knowing one is 'un lache des laches'.* (Foot, op.cit)

Trix never knew until much later that the wireless set dropped with her was retrieved and used to send messages back to London. C. J. Smit, her rendezvous, and his friend were arrested at the address in The Hague she gave Poos and Slagter. They were shot the following year.

Given the number and density of anti-aircraft artillery in the Low Countries very few of the Tempsford planes returned. It is said that orders were issued to shoot at them on their return flight so their passengers and contents could be dropped safely. As has been mentioned, twelve were shot down over the winter of 1942-3.

Nel Lind, a fellow prisoner at Haaren, said that she had the impression that the Germans wanted to keep Trix alive. They even gave her a wireless with which she could listen to the BBC whilst she was in solitary confinement. Apart from a brief spell when they unsuccessfully planted another girl in her cell as a stool pigeon, someone to whom Trix was supposed to tell her real story to, she was alone for eighteen months,

One wonders whether her training prepared her for such an eventuality.

Foot mentions prisoners tapping Morse messages to each other on water pipes and news of eight agents' capture reaching MI6. Their telegram to the SOE in June 1943 was disregarded but confirmation didn't reach N section until November. Two SOE agents had managed to escape from Haaren in August and were escorted down one of the escape lines, crossed into Switzerland and in November sent a full report to London revealing the scale of the disaster. managed to get back to England. As Giskes sent London a message telling them that two double agents had escaped, their stories were doubted and it was weeks before they were eventually released from interrogation. (DVD 'Secret War - Episode 7 The Dutch Disaster', Athena, 2011) However, no plans were put in place to help Trix and the other Englandspiel victims escape or to stop any further agents being dropped.

Diet Eman, in her book, *Things We Couldn't Say,* recalls her time in Haaren where she met Trix who, she said,

> "*wore a tiny piece of fur round her neck that resembled a* (pine) *marten. She called it "Freddy" and sometimes spoke to it and stroked it... Her eyes seemed kind of wild and nervous, very sunken, and her facial features were pulled tight. She was very anxious.*
>
> *That night, after the others had gone to sleep, I stayed awake because something inside me told me that this woman was special. Although I'd never met her before, my instincts told me I could trust her, and I knew there was more to her than the little, she'd told us. We sat on the floor against the wall, just the*

two of us, and we talked the whole night while the others were asleep. She told me her story that night in cell 306.

She was from a very well-to-do family, so rich that she didn't have to have a job. Before the war she had studied at university, but she became bored with going to school, she said. Air travel had just begun at that time, and she became one of the KLM airline's first stewardesses. She said that she flew only to challenge herself: she had been deathly afraid of flying, so she challenged herself to get on an airplane by becoming a stewardess, of all things.

When war broke out, she'd made her way to England and was working for the Dutch intelligence service. When she arrived, Queen Wilhelmina invited Beatrix over for tea! It's difficult for Americans to understand loyalty and love for the crown, but I always loved our royal family. That night, when Beatrix told me that she had had tea with the queen, I was nearly overwhelmed with admiration for her!

During the questioning of Schreieder after the war, Trix admitted that he had attended to a complaint she made about food in prison which resulted in all the *Englandspiel* prisoners' diets being improved.

A fellow inmate, Mrs Parmintier, wrote a coded letter to a contact in Lisbon for her husband, the content of which attracted the attention of the censors. They were concerned that she named some members of the resistance. Dated 25 March 1944, she intimated that Trix had been executed by the Germans at Amersfoot. (TNA HS 6/762) SOE didn't get to see it until Captain Parmentier, a KLM pilot, reached England, by which time they knew different.

After fifteen months at Haaren, she was sent to

Scheveningen prison, known as the 'Orange Hotel' because of the number of Dutch resistance members held there.

On May 7 1944 she was transferred to Ravensbrück, a Nazi concentration camp opened in May 1939, primarily for women and children. It was located in a beauty spot about fifty miles (80 km) north of Berlin and noted for its lakes and secluded villas for wealthy city-dwellers. Its site was on marshy ground, often infested with malarial mosquitoes. There were enclaves outside the camp for working parties doing factory or heavy agricultural work in the community, as well as a Jugendlager, or youth camp, where those too ill or unfit for work were accommodated.

In Beryl Escott's *Mission Improbable,* an account of fifteen women in the WAAF (Women's Auxilliary Air Force) sent into France, she gave a long account which is worth including. It gives you an idea of the conditions many of the women and girls had to endure, one of whom, Anne Frank, found posthumous fame through her diary,

> *The main camp surrounded by high walls was built for about 6,000 prisoners. Inside were wooden huts for living quarters containing three tiers of bunks, a few brick buildings for kitchens, showers and a concrete cell block. Cinder paths divided the huts in front of which blossomed flowers in profusion. But there, all semblance of cleanliness and proper conditions stopped. The place was in fact known to the French as L'Enfer des Femmes, the Women's Hell.*
>
> *Nearly all the prisoners were civilians, both young and old, from conquered countries either as*

slave labour or on suspicion of involvement with the resistance, all being imprisoned without trial, though this did not prevent them being cruelly tortured during questioning in the camp's political department. During the war years over 50,000 women, at the lowest estimate, died in this camp from dirt, disease, overcrowding, squalor, starvation, overwork and ill-treatment, apart from those who were shot or gassed or sent to die elsewhere.

When Cécile Lefort was admitted in 1943, she spent her first days in the quarantine hut, where new arrivals were kept for three weeks to ensure they brought no new infection to the camp. After being checked in, though weary from the long train journey, she had to stand several hours before being admitted to the bathhouse, where she was told to strip and her former clothes were taken away. Here she waited naked in the cold for a further few hours under the tiny hole in the ceiling where the shower worked, and that was only for a few minutes. With a sliver of soap and a pocket handkerchief of a towel she had to clean herself. Again a long wait and then a shock. Two men came in, one to look at her teeth and one to give her a cursory medical examination, which revealed something was wrong.

Then she was issued with prison clothing, thin and inadequate for the advancing winter, and dispatched to the quarantine hut. There, no one was to be allowed outside, though all were awakened well before dawn for bitter acorn coffee. They were crowded at the window watching while the other women lined up five deep in front of their huts, in the freezing cold and rain, the living and the dead together, and stood for the hour-long 'Appells', where they were counted and appointed their work for the day. Some were detailed for gardening, some for sewing or knitting, some for corpse, rubbish or coal collecting, some for road mending, cleaning latrines, tree-felling or potato picking, women being used instead of horses to drag the heavy carts. Work went in shifts of 10 or 11 hours each, day and night, lights out coming at about 9 pm. Food, mainly vegetable soup and half a loaf of bread a day, was not sufficient for such heavy work. This was the life that awaited them when quarantine was finished. (Escott, B. (1991), *Mission Improbable,* Sparkford: Patrick Stephens Limited)

Neave says that Trix suffered appallingly in health and mind, being told initially that she would be exchanged for captured German prisoners-of-war. In January 1945 she was transferred to the Mauthausen-Gosen concentration camp. It was from here that she and Lauwers were eventually liberated by American forces on May 5, 1945. All the other inmates had been executed or died. The experience ruined her health. Neave's postscript of her story reads:

She has never indulged in any recrimination and bitterness. She has treated her nightmarish experience as one of the fortunes of war. It was this quiet faith and serenity of spirit which brought admiration from her captors. Thanks to her refusal to talk, she was one of the few survivors of 'Northpole' who escaped death.

As she wrote to me afterwards:

"I was an amateur but in war risks have to be taken. I played a game of cat and mouse with the Gestapo with the only difference that I was caged and the cat was free. (Neave, op.cit)

In the last note in her personnel file, dated 22 June 1945, Neave wrote to Captain W. E. Mills, their representative in Utrecht informing him of a change of plan. London had informed him that Trix was fit to leave hospital in Switzerland and able to travel to England by the second week in July instead of the original plan that she went to Nijmeden. He also said that he'd made arrangements to contact her parents and keep them informed. The last note in her personal file was from H. J. Philips of Unilever House, dated 27 August 1945, acknowledging receipt from the War Office of four of Trix's suitcases and an envelope of keys.

In recognition of Trix's experiences in attempting to help the Dutch in their struggle for liberation, a number of streets were named in her honour in Rotterdam, Spijkenisse, Sassenheim, Leiden and Middelburg. Her autobiography, 'Een Vrouw Vloog Mee, was published in 1951.

It was almost eighteen months after Trix was parachuted in before the next woman was dropped into Holland. Jelle Hoolveld, a military historian, gave me the names of the two other women agents, Antonia Hamilton and Jos Gemmeke. They were said to have been in the *Bureau Bijzondere Opdrachten* (BBO), which translates as the Bureau of Special Operations)

On 10 August 1944, a month before the battle of Arnhem, Flight Lieutenant Terence Helfer of 161 Squadron, took off from Tempsford at 0018 hours in his Hudson. Despite poor visibility, at 0204 hours he dropped Antonia and her brother

Frank Hamilton with a container of weapons and two pigeons near Abbekerk, a rural community about two miles (5km) north of Hoorn and twenty kilometres northeast of Alkmaar. Given the previous disasters, they were dropped blind, without a reception committee.

Their personal files in the National Archives provided fascinating details of their missions. Whilst in training in Britain, Antonia was known as Josephine. In line with the names of games N Section was then using for its agents sent into Holland, hers was TIDDLEYWINKS and Frank's was ROWING. In the field her codename was HEMERIK. Frank's name in the field was Frans Hertog and his codename was GUUS. (TNA HS 6/767)

When they arrived at the barn at Gibraltar Farm Form A.T.F. 7 had to be taken from the desk. This was the list of equipment agents were to be issued with. Antonia's was stamped MOST SECRET and dated 26 July 1944. It gave her height as 1m. 72 and her weight 125 pounds, information valuable for the issuing officer who would be able to locate all these items on the three-foot (1 m) wide concrete shelves which ran around the inside of the building. She was given a Colt .32 revolver with fifty rounds of ammunition, a locking knife, a pocket compass, field dressings, a torch with one spare battery and bulb, a pack of Lyons emergency rations and a flask of Cognac. Over her ordinary clothes she had a striptease parachutist's suit, harness, parachute, an old type helmet, spine, knees and heel pads, ankle bandages, overboots and a spade to bury the parachute after she landed. The 'L' pill was not issued but she took four 'B' tablets, Benzedrine, to help keep her awake.

Her mission papers, also dated 26 July, read:

MOST SECRET

ORDERS FOR: HEMERIK

INFORMATION

HANS contacted the Clandestine Press in April 1944, gave them money and delivered a special message from H.M. The Queen of the Netherlands to the Clandestine Press. Unfortunately on landing, HANS and his operator FRANS, lost their W/T material. After completing his mission HANS returned to this country to arrange delivery of new W/T material.

While HANS was returning FRANS managed to send us a few messages on another operator's W/T set. We attempted to send new material but the aircraft was lost. FRANS gave us particulars of a dropping ground called TULIP but as this ground and the B.B.C. messages were mentioned in a message from another organisation, we fear that it may no longer be safe and too well-known to too many people and possibly even to the Gestapo.

HANS left in charge a certain PEITER DEKKER, but no messages have been received from FRANS or PIETER since 27 June. The following are possible reasons: -

That the other organisation, on instructions, broke contact with FRANS, leaving him without communication

That FRANS has got into trouble.

That the other organisation has got into or was in trouble and that FRANS broke contact with them and is keeping low or trying to make his escape.

Operation Name

The name of your operation is TIDDLYWINKS and you will be known by this name at the station of your departure. You will never use this name when you are in the field.

<u>Code Names in the Field</u>

Your field name will be Josephine: this is the only name you or your partner should use in messages from the field, and it is the name by which you will be known by other members of the organisation. The operational code of your partner is ROWING, and his name in the field will be GUUS.

<u>INTENTION</u>

You will be sent to Holland to contact (See Annexe I), and after having satisfied him as to your bona-fides, you will explain the above information to him and ask him to find out whether or not PIETER DEKKER (See Annexe II) is still all right, and if so, to put you in touch with him. When you have contacted PEITER, you will tell him that HANS is safe in this country, to deliver to him the propaganda material, Hfl. 25,000 and the material for FRANS, if he is still all right. The propaganda material contains a message from H.M. The Queen of the Netherlands for the Clandestine Press. You will tell PIETER that in addition to delivering the above, your mission is to assist the Clandestine Press in their photography work and that GUUS is to act as reception committee leader.

PIETER has asked for a quicker method of sending their films to us - you will explain the method of despatch by pigeon, but that failing delivery of pigeons, the films can be collected at PARIS. It is for the Clandestine Press to give us an address and password in PARIS, where we can collect. You can tell us this through FRANS, but failing W/T contact, you will send it to us embodied in an innocent letter, together with details of the dropping point. It will be well to duplicate or even triplicate innocent letters and to send them on different dates and in different texts and handwriting.

You will tell PIETER that, as you and GUUS have not been in HOLLAND for some considerable time, he must arrange for you both to live underground and to arrange for your safe house.
It is most important that, no matter how much you may be persuaded to contact people or confide in them, you will keep to your mission and make no contacts other than those arranged for you by PIETER.
If your initial contact as per Annexe I informs you that something has gone wrong with PIETER, you may then hand him the money, the propaganda material, and the Queen's message, and suggest that you continue your mission with him or with any other safe Clandestine Press group t his discretion. You will hand to PIETER or your initial contact, if PIETER is not safe, a microfilm relative to listening posts in HOLLAND, as per Annexe III. GUUS will take steps to organise a Reception Committee to receive such Stores as he may request to be sent to him.
METHOD
On the first favourable night in the July/August moon period, you and GUUS will be dropped together at a point which will be explained to you prior to your departure. Immediately on landing, you will bury your parachute and equipment; the packages, containing two suitcases will be buried separately and, if possible, in such a place as can easily be recognised, so that it may be collected by a third party as we do not wish you to endanger yourselves by carrying it around. If you wish, you may bury your revolver with the package.. (Ibid.)

She had been given a list of the contents of both suitcases. The black one for Pieter Dekker contained seven "clichés series A to E, and P to Q", two "A Mk III's" (the latest radio sets), a vibrator pack, ten crystals and plan and two "O.T.P.'s" (One=Time-Pads), one camera and six films of Kodak 35, copies of *The Times*, a film of the invasion of France, a set of stamps and two copies of the Queen Wilhelmina's speech of 6 December 1942. These latter documents had been specifically asked for by Dekker. Her brown suitcase contained a Kodak 35 camera and four films, full equipment for microphotography, one pair of shoes, her clothes and German propaganda.

> *<u>Contacts</u>*
> *Initial contact on landing, se Annexe I, which will also be the initial contact of the organisation.*
> *<u>Residence</u>*
> *This will be looked after by the organisation to which you are being sent.*

<u>ADMINISTRATION</u>

> *GUUS will take with him the sum of Hfl. 25,000, the disposal of which has been dealt with in the "INTENTION". You will also have Hfl. 5,000 for your own use, and your partner will have the same sum. You will each have as well Ffrs. 2,500, and Bfrs. 2,500 for use, should you require it in an emergency.*
> *<u>Package - Equipment - Camouflage</u>*
> *Your personal baggage will consist of one handbag.*
> *You will be supplied with Hfl. 200.00 in small change for your immediate needs.*
> *The remainder of your personal money viz. Hfl. 4,800 and Ffrs. 2,500 and Bfrs. 2,500 is in your money belt. The Hfls. 25,000 will be carried in a money belt by GUUS.*
> *GUUS will also have the sum of Hfl. 5,000, Ffrs 2,500 and Bfrs. 2,500 on his person.*

> *Your code (a twelve page One Time Pad) is camouflaged as per Annexe IV.*
>
> *A package will be parachuted with you. This will consist of two suitcases; one suitcase contains W/T equipment and propaganda material destined for PIETER DEKKER as per the "INTENTION", the other suitcase contains your clothing, camera and micro-photography equipment. This latter suitcase will be specially marked..* (Ibid.)

The cover story she was given was as close to the truth as possible. Should she be captured and interrogated, she needed to know the story off by heart. The name on her identity card was *Antonia Wouters*, born on 22 May 1910 at Breda. She grew up at Ginnekeweg 8 and was known to everyone as 'Ton'. Her parents, Anton and Hendrika, were both Dutch and their dates of birth were provided. Her father was a wood broker and her mother a housewife. It detailed which schools she went to and that she helped around the house when she left. From October 1930 until summer 1932 she worked as a housekeeper for Mrs. van Oerle of Oegstgeesterweg 8 in Lieden but when her parents decided, for business reasons, to emigrate to America, she went with them. They lived at 444 Central Park West in New York. Mr. Wouters engaged in the wood trade with various American business men.

Aged only twenty-two when she was in America, 'Ton' did very little work, just lived off her father's earnings. In 1934 she got engaged to Derek van der Linden but he broke it off in summer 1938. Heart-broken and rather tired of the Americans, she decided to return to Holland. Despite her parents not being keen on it, she was an adult and was determined to leave. The SOE had done their homework. They had gone to the trouble of contacting various shipping agencies to get the correct details for her cost of return tickets from

Rotterdam to New York. She sailed on the S.S. Volendam of the Amerika Line in a cabin which cost £69 in 1932 and £65.10s.0d. in 1938. The prices for Tourist class return tickets for the same years were £43.5s.0d and £50.15s.0d. and 3 class £33.5s.0d. and £38.10s.0d. They even provided all the dates she needed to convince anyone making enquiries about her travel arrangements.

'Ton' went to work at a friend of her father's in Amsterdam, Dr. H. J. Damen of Prinsengracht 1019. In return for looking after the house, she was paid a little but her father had given her sufficient funds to be quite comfortably off. She stayed there during the war until she was called up by the Arbeidsdienst (Employment Bureau) and ordered to work as a kitchen inspector in the Oorlogstijd Afdeeling Massa Voedeing (Wartime Mass Feeding Programme) in Amsterdam. How and when she go to England was not documented.

The relevant documents, a Legitimatiebewijs Voedselvoorziening in Oorlogstijd and a Dutch Identity Card were provided. She had previously been interviewed by an officer regarding the use of neutral post-boxes and passwords. Camouflaged in her handbag were a one-time pad, documents for the journey from Holland to France in case of emergency and a W.O.K. (Worked Out Key) Code. Other information she was provided with covered:

COMMUNICATION

<u>In the Field</u>

You will use the various methods which have been taught you for communication between yourself, your partner and members of your organisation: post-boxes, cut-outs etc. you may also arrange various danger signals.

b) <u>Wireless</u>

FRANS, in due course, will act as your W/T operator. He is in possession of his own code, but you will do all the encoding and decoding of our messages to and from you: this must be strictly adhered to for the security of all concerned. You must inform FRANS of your prefixes, see Annexe VII.
c) Messages by W/T
In order to maintain the security of your W/T operator, it is essential that your messages should be kept as short as possible and limited to important information connected with your mission. Records of messages exchanged should not be kept.
d) Innocent letters
(i) Code: You will use the convention which you have been taught. See Annexe VIII.
(ii) Address: You will send your Innocent Letter to an address as per Annexe IX.
(iii) Signatures: You will sign your innocent Letters Josephine, and if we write we will sign KOOS.
B.B.C. Messages
On the first, second and third days and on the two following Sundays, we shall broadcast as per Annexe X. this will prove your bona-fide.
Emergency Address
It is important that we should remain in contact with you, and, if possible, you should give us an address before you leave for the field. If you are unable to do this, you should let us have the address at the first possible moment by W/T. (Ibid.)

The address she was given for Frans was Miss Meerman, Concierge Peace Palace, The Hague and the password she had to use was "*I bring you greetings from Harmen Dijkstar*" to which the response had to be "*Excellent, please come inside.*" She was told that, should she or her brother lose each other on landing, they had to meet at the address of Jos Gemmeke. There was also an instruction about security:

> *If we have reason to suppose that you have been arrested and that the Germans are working the transmitter, we will ask you an "innocent" question. If you are safe, you will give us the correct answer, but if we do not receive the correct answer we shall presume that you are in enemy hands.*
>
> 5. *FINANCIAL ARRANGEMENTS*
> *Your salary will be credited to your account with the Dutch government.* (Ibid.)

The description she was given of Pieter Dekker was that he was approximately 28 years old, 1m. 80 in height with a small face, smooth dark blonde hair, combed back. He had a long nose, had a thin body, walked unusually, was well dressed and sometimes wore glasses as a camouflage. Interestingly, his contact address was Jos Gemmeke, Amalia van Solmsstraat 119, DEN HAAG. Jos Gemmeke will appear later.

The description of her first contact, Guardmaster de Vries, which she had to memorise, was that he was approximately 45 years old. His height was given as 1m. 76. He had thin light darkish fair hair. His eyes were light in colour. He looked people straight in the eyes. Sometimes he dressed as a farmer in working clothes with a cap hanging over one side of his head. At other times he wore uniform. He had a round face, was not thick-set and spoke very carefully, even, and it was underlined, that he pretends that he is wrong in the beginning when you first meet him. What she was also provided with was his contact details and a bit of background information.

> *Guardmaster DE VRIES (Chief of Police) Santpoortdorp, Broekbergenlaan 15. The names are on the gate (See accompanying drawing).*
> *I've just come from TOBS, who is far away. You will remember that he gave you money for the investigation into the BRABANT case. When TOBS left the last time it was a pity that he could not take your brother-in-law with him. Do you remember the marigold campaign with our friend who lives next door to NIJSSEN?*
> *Guardmaster DE VRIES must send somebody. You must not go by yourself.*
> *Neither FRANS nor Pieter DEKKER knows how to reach DE VRIES. JOSEPHINE must ask DE VRIES if he is willing to investigate whether there's been any penetration by the German Police in TOBS' absence.*
> *DE VRIES knows FRANS and probably knows how to reach him.*
> *JOSEPHINE must ask for shelter during the time that Guardmaster DE VRIES takes to do his quick investigation.*
> *As soon as Guardmaster DE VRIES knows if No. 90 is safe, shelter needs to be found during the time of the investigation in THE HAGUE.*
> *Guardmaster DE VRIES is obviously suspicious and will most probably ask trick questions.*
> *The connection between HAARLEM and SANTIPOORT is good (See accompanying drawing).* (Ibid.)

Hidden in her brother Frank's belongings was a microfilm containing the details of twenty drop zones. It gave their code names, different types of fish, the signal letter for the Eureka direction finding beacon, the S-Phone (ground to air radio communication) codenames as well as the BBC messages that indicated the mission was on. After the 1900 hours news on Radio Oranje, a list of phrases were read out. This meant the mission was planned. If the same message was read out after the 2100 hours news, it meant the mission was definitely on and the reception committee should get in place. For example COD's signal letter was A, the S-Phone call was NASSAU to ORANGE and the BBC message was HET HEEFT EEN WEEK GEDUURD. Additional information included standby times for the next moon period, vital for the coming invasion. Between 28 August and 5 September they were to be from 2100 to 0100 G.M.T. but that from 6 September until the 11th they were to be from 2300 to 0300 G.M.T. One wonders if she queried what the significance of 5 September 1944 was.

It was *Dolle Dinstag,* Mad Tuesday, the day when an exuberant population came out onto the streets waving orange flags, waiting expectantly for the Allied armies to drive up from Belgium and liberate them. Operation MARKET GARDEN was a plan to cross the Meuse, Wall and Rhine rivers into Holland but it came to a halt at the well-defended bridge at Arnhem. By early-December the German bridgehead between the Meuse and the Peel marshes had been defeated but much of northern Holland stayed in German occupation until late-March 1945.

Some historians claim that the *Englandspiel* provided the Germans with a strategic advantage in Holland, that of significantly delaying the organisation and arming of an active Dutch resistance, potentially contributing to the Allies advance from Belgium into Holland getting stuck at Arnhem.

Those Dutch people desperate for news about the Allies advances could turn on their wireless set and tune into the broadcasts of Radio Oranje, the official radio station of the government in exile. However, many more tuned into De

Flitspuit, a short-wave radio station which broadcast black propaganda. It was less formal and many people thought it was broadcast in Holland. Although listening to both these stations was illegal, most people did so secretly. When it broadcast an order from the government in exile for all railway workers to go on strike on 18 September 1944 word got round so fast that all trains were stopped by midnight. Foot mentioned that all Dutch civilian railway traffic didn't restart until after the Germans surrendered in May 1945.

> *Most railway workers dijkten onder, went underground; all received strike pay, most of it supplied secretly from London from the earnings of the Dutch mercantile marine. Not a doppeltje, not a farthing went astray.*
>
> *The appalling consequence had not been foreseen by Gerbrandy* (the Dutch Prime Minister), *who gave the order;...The Germans brought in their own railwaymen to move and supply their own troops, traffic to sustain Dutch civilians had to go by road or by barge, and as a reprisal to the strike the Germans thereupon banned barge traffic. The horrors of the Hunger Winter, still unforgotten, followed: ending in nearly sixteen thousand deaths from starvation, in one of the most fertile countries on earth.* (Foot, op.cit. p.396)

What was also included in Antonia's file was a document entitled 'STENTOR MISSION FOR THE NETHERLANDS'. To give you a better understanding of the Allies' plans prior to the invasion of Holland it has been included in the Appendix.

Reminders about her security might have included being told to read a British government publication aimed at service personnel going into Holland. What follows is part of the advice given to those sent into Norway but the message would have been equally important for Antonia.

> *SECURITY NOTE*
> *Now is the time for you to realise that all that you have learned about security during your training at home applies with equal measure to operations overseas.... One of the most important reasons for this is that you have moved and will continue to move into areas which have been occupied by the Enemy for a long time.*
> ***The Enemy will spare no pains to leave behind, scattered among the civilian population, agents, saboteurs and propagandists who will be a continued threat to our security.***
> *Their numbers will greatly exceed anything with which we have had to cope in the past - and it will be infinitely more difficult to detect them. Added to this, the Enemy will have prepared channels of communication for the use of his agents, which he may well be able to use long after actual hostilities have ceased.*
> ***So there must be no relaxation of security-mindedness and suspicious alertness, even in those areas where the battle has moved on and comparatively peaceful conditions may prevail. In these areas particularly you must be on your guard.***
> *As you have been told so often, personal responsibility is the key-note of good security. ...* ***Do not forget that more Europeans understand English than is popularly supposed. So be very careful what you say - not only to civilians, but to each other in their hearing.*** *You should keep a particular look-out for suspects, and report immediately any cases which you come across ... Pay particular attention to the checking of identity documents*

and do not hesitate to detain, if necessary by force, any suspicious individuals. Some of these may be disguised as British officers or men; and it is not unlikely that the beautiful spy will come into her own again.
The dangers of sabotage will also be considerable. This means that when you are guarding material or equipment, your job will be particularly important; and that you must continue to take great care of your personal weapons and equipment.
You must expect that propaganda will be directed to driving a wedge between the Allies, for instance by attempts to promote anti-Russian feeling. There may also be attempts to organise sympathy for the German people. This propaganda, which may be in many forms - some crude and obvious, but some subtle and hard to recognise - will be directed by enemy sympathisers and agents against your morale. Women are clever at this sort of work, and will no doubt often be used. Do not allow yourself to be affected by any of this. You have a job to do - and you must see it through with good will and determination.
Life in ex-German Europe will demand your vigilance, alertness and self-confidence. These must be used in applying with common-sense the security principles you have been taught. ('Norway', British Government Wartime publication)

Antonia's mission was to re-establish propaganda links and send messages to the underground press on behalf of Queen Wilhelmina but, as it turned out, the mission did not go ahead as planned. Why? They both landed in a canal! She broke both her tibia and fibula in her leg. Despite the pain she managed, with Frank's help to reach a nearby farmhouse where she hid for a couple of nights. A few days later the Dutch resistance arrived and took her to Haarlem via Alkmaar where she was put in hospital under a false name. The flask of Cognac would have come in handy to dull the pain until she got to see a doctor.

According to Foot, her brother, though much distressed at her injury, ensured that she was well treated and accommodated in a safe farmhouse with Tobias Biallosterski, another Dutch SOE agent, Codenamed *Draughts 2*, he had been among the first batch of agents dropped into Holland following RAF agreeing to resume flights in the late March and early April moon period. He was dropped for his second mission on 8/9 September east of Aalkmaar to act initially as a link-man between the Dutch government in exile and the Raad van Verzet and then with Prince Bernhard who was in residence with Princess Julienne in their country palace at Soestdijk. According to Foot, Biallosterski organised North Holland so well that he was able to import arms for over a thousand men into Amsterdam, hidden in the false bottom of a barge. Whether Antonia played any part in his work is unknown,

She couldn't walk properly until after the Germans had surrendered the following year. Whether she managed to undertake all her mission is unknown. It is more than likely that Frank took them on. He is described in the N section history as having done '*an extremely good job in North Holland Province, training a large number of potential instructors in sabotage and reception committee work.*'

After the war Ton and her brother put in an expenses claim for 10,000 Dutch florins. The exchange rate at the time was ten florins to the pound. On 28 July 1945 Captain W. E. Mills of Special Forces HQ in Montagu Mansions on Montagu Street, London W.1, wrote to Captain K. de Graaf of 1 Konigalaan, Utrecht, asking him to obtain confirmation from the various people the Hamiltons owed money to. Ton claimed 1,000 florins for her transport from her hiding place in Ubbekerk to Almaar-Santpoort-Haarlem and the second time when she went back to Alkmaar for control. She wanted 400 florins to pay Dick Waalder and his family who looked after her at her first hiding place. They bought her warm winter clothes, provided fuel for her room, medicine, bandages and nourishing food. 500 florins was asked for her food until 16 September, 1,600 for the Marine Hospital in Alkmaar for her stay there, massage and bandages from 16 September until 29 January 1945.

To confirm that her stay afterwards was in a room in Santpoort, opposite the station, she provided them with the names of several people who would vouch for her. They included Flock, Haverskamp, who she added was killed, Dr. Wamstiker, the surgeon and his assistant Dr Glasenburg., A further 1,800 guilders was asked for clothing, food and massage when she was in hiding from 9 February until 8 May, and 800 for food between 8 and 27 May, SOE had promised both of them a further 5,000 florins which, they claimed, they never received.

The contact address where Antonia was supposed to find Pieter Dekker mentioned Jos Gemmeke. In Frans Kluiters' list of Dutch Agents 1940 - 1945 and Foot's *The SOE in the Low Countries,* they both mention 22-year-old Jos Gemmeke. Born on 3 June 1922, she lived with her parents and sister in The Hague and on May 10 1940 watched from the balcony of the family house the first bombing of the city. At the beginning of the war she worked as an auxiliary nurse in the Westeinde hospital but then got a job in the International Court of Justice.

In an interview after the war included on the *Radio Nederland Wereldomroep* website she said that it was through a friend that she was put in contact with the resistance. She was so mad that the Germans just marched in, took over the country and began the persecution and deportation of the Jews.

Her father was a paper merchant and the first man she ever worked for turned out to be the editor of '*Je Maintiendrai*', one of the greatest underground newspapers. Its title was the motto under the Dutch coat of arms which translates as 'I will persevere'. Her work involved helping with the printing and distribution of 25,000 copies., activities which, if she had been caught by the Germans, would have meant death. In fact, she did it so well that she looked after several other journals' distribution as well. Only the *Civil Contakt* in Santpoort had an larger circulation.

She admitted that she had been involved with resistance activities from the very beginning of the occupation, building up an entire network of contacts and, for security, was known by them all, not as Jos Gemmeke, but as *Els von Dalen*. '*You didn't think about being a woman at that time. That was not important ... they needed people and I wanted to help, I couldn't do anything else.*' (Mulder-Gemmeke, J. 12297, IWMSA)

One of her friends, Cock of Easter Chen, lived downstairs in the Peace Palace, where his mother was the principal supervisor. On Friday nights they would go into the attic with a heavy mimeograph, a machine for stencil printing papers. They spent the whole weekend printing out copies ready for distribution on Monday. Taking them on the train in a suitcase she admitted was dangerous work but girls had less chance of being caught. Flirting with the Germans meant that they were more courteous when she was carrying her case.

Later on she worked as a communications officer, carrying wireless equipment and other goods dropped for the Dutch resistance by Tempsford's 138 Squadron. Whether she met Antonia, Frank or Tobias Biallosterski is unknown. In an interview for Elsevier Magazine after the war she admitted that she took on the most dangerous assignments like smuggling pistols and radio sets and helping take people hiding from the Germans down the escape line towards Belgium because '*she was a person who liked to take others under her wings*.' All this gave her what she called a sixth sense for danger and betrayal.

On September 5, there was the expectation that it only be a matter of time before the Allies liberated the whole country. Tens of thousands of Germans and Dutch collaborators desperately tried to leave but, to the disappointment of the resistance, they returned when they learned that the Allies' advance from Belgium into Holland had ground to a halt. Operation MARKET GARDEN failed to capture the bridges over the Meuse, Waal and Lower Rhine.

According to Eddy de Roever, whose biography of Jos, *Sphinx,* narrates her wartime experiences, this was despite the resistance giving valuable information to the Allies. Patience and determination was needed.

In October 1944 a radio message was sent to the Allies on the front line asking them to send a messenger to occupied Holland. Prince Bernhard needed someone to take some important documents to Brussels for him, The British refused to send a plane, arguing that there was nowhere safe for a Lysander or a Hudson pickup. Somebody had to go from the occupied north to the liberated south of Holland so Jos volunteered. One of her friends, a doctor, was working in a hospital where German officers were being treated. He arranged for one of them to sign a number of documents, one of which was Jos's travel permit. He also taught her how to simulate a nervous breakdown, in case she was captured.

On 23 October 1944, on a bicycle with one rubber tyre the

other made of wood, she cycled out of The Hague with the vital microfilms safely tucked away, They contained details of German troop numbers and the location of the V1 and V2 rocket launch sites in Groningen.

One of the farmers told her that she would not be able to cross the Meuse as the Germans were turning everybody back. She ignored him but was then unlucky enough to be on the road when Allied bombers were strafing the German vehicles. They came round six times but she avoided the bullets. In the commotion she found herself amongst tired, bearded SS and Wehrmacht troops. (de Roever, E. (1987), *Sphinx: het verhaal van Jos Gemmeke*, Hollandia Publishers, Baarn)

In an interview on the *oorlogsgetuigen* website she said that, despite being shot at by British planes as she made her way south through enemy lines, she managed to charm a *Feldwebel* into allowing her to cross the River Waal into Belgium.

> *It was extremely difficult to arrange getting on the ferry in Gorinchem. When I got to the bridge by Heusden, I wasn't allowed to cross there either. Then, during an attack by the Allied Air Force, all the German soldiers fled from the bridge so I was finally able to cross over. But it was raining bullets.* (http://www.oorlogsgetuigen.nl/Silence)

As she approached the front line she suddenly found herself amongst a group of Scottish POWs, guarded by heavily armed Germans. Near the town of Vught her bicycle was destroyed by shrapnel. Afterwards she could not remember how she survived or had the courage to continue. "It was as if an invisible hand protected me".

At the first pre-arranged hiding place she was in the middle of the fighting which continued all night. There were enormous explosions all around her, machine gun fire and people screaming for help. As dawn approached the fighting got less intense until it became frighteningly silent. The family hiding her climbed out of the cellar. There was not a German in sight. Suddenly she heard someone call "*Hello. Don't be afraid*". It was a soldier with a cigarette in his mouth and a Sten gun nonchalantly carried over his shoulder.

On 26 October, despite the occasional sniper bullets, a motor-courier managed to take her on the back of his motorbike to Eindhoven. Several Allied officers, amongst then Dutch officers under Allied command, tried to persuade Jos to hand over the documents but she refused. She would only give them to Prince Bernhard, her Commander-in-Chief.

She reached Brussels by car on 28 October she delivered the microfilm hidden in her powder compact and the important papers hidden in her shoulder pads to him personally. In appreciation, she was invited to dinner with him and his staff officers, eating and drinking what she had not been able to for more than four years. There was even pink champagne which Jos had never even heard of before.

When she asked to be able to return to The Hague, she was refused as it was too dangerous. When she insisted she was given three choices - to go back via England, to work at the HQ of the BBO in London or to stay and work at their HQ in The Hague. She chose the first option but then had to wait for an airplane. In *Sphinx,* Eddy de Roever's biography of Gemmeke, he mentions

The only way to return to The Hague from Brussels was via England, and then only by parachute... So I went to England because I wanted as soon as possible to return to

> *the Netherlands to continue the fight. From the beginning of the war I was always extremely security-minded. I denied everything and never wrote anything down. The whole war no one knew my real name. Because of this caution, I survived.* (de Roever, op.cit.)

As the documents she had brought were destined for the Bureau Bijzondere Opdrachten, the Dutch Intelligence Service in London, Prince Bernhard arranged for her to be flown to Croydon, south London, on 31 October. For security reasons she travelled in the green-painted Dakota under the name of *Jeanne Guersen.*

She was met by a friendly lieutenant and a FANY driver took her straight to the Royal Patriotic School for questioning. After two days of obligatory interrogations, repeating answers to questions to determine whether or not she was a German agent, she gave them a telephone number to ring that she had been given in Brussels. It worked and on 2 November she was released. A Dutch colonel called van Oorschot drove her in his military staff car to his office in Park Street, where, according to de Roever, she was devastated to be told that the SOE had forbidden female agents from being dropped in enemy occupied territory.

The FANY driver took her to an apartment in Lancaster Gate where she was able to stay. To keep up her cover story she had to join the FANY and, to keep herself busy, she worked for the signalling section.

By the end of January 1945 she was told that "Baker Street" wanted to parachute her back into Holland. On 4 February she was driven down to Beaulieu for the SOE's 'Finishing School'. Foot refers to her officers describing her as *"a very level and cool-headed young woman, completely unemotional, very reserved and very determined."* (Foot,

(2001),op.cit.) The major in charge came over to Jos and told her that she was the best student the section had ever had in the four years of operations.

On 24 February she was taken for her parachute training at Ringway and she remembered jumping from Whitley bombers into the grounds of Tatton Park and staying at Altringham. This was Dunham House (STS 51a). Her jump instructor was called Captain Can and he was so worried about Jos that he always was by her side when she made a jump. As the training intensified the jumps had to be made from increasing heights. She had weak ankles and because she was worried about getting a fracture after her exercise-jumps, she tried to land on her "bottom" which caused so much pain that moving, sitting or lying down was impossible. She had to be treated by a doctor which meant no jumps for a long time. Jos was lucky because the weather got so bad that her group could not do any jumps either so that she did not lose time. Their 'graduation' party was in the 'King's Arms' pub on or about 1 March.

During the first week in March she was prepared for her mission at Park Street and Baker Street by officers in the SOE, BBO and OSS. On the 6 March, a message was sent from London to a radio operator in Holland telling them that Sphinx was coming. Before she left, her Commander told her that he admired her bravery, being prepared to go back into enemy occupied Belgium.

With the code name *Cackle*, she was driven in a blacked out car to an isolated airfield at Waterbeach, just north of Cambridge. Why the flight was not from Tempsford where most of the other SOE, SIS and OSS flights left from, I have not been able to determine. Maybe there had been a technical problem on take off which meant the pilot had to make an emergency landing at Waterbeach.

Her personal belongings were packed into one of the weapons containers that were being dropped with her. After donning all her parachute equipment and being given supplies for her mission, she was given a final briefing before boarding a converted Short Stirling bomber. The pilot is said to have protested at having to take someone so young. She was only twenty-two. When he recognised how brave she was, he put his hand on her shoulder and promised to get her to the reception committee.

Most of her personal belongings were stowed in the containers that were to be dropped with her. The important documents she kept on her. In the hurry to get her on board she did not have her Mae West life jacket or parachute on. She thought that there would be plenty of time for her to put them on during the flight.

In de Roever's book he described it as a cold and stormy night. Crossing the Dutch North Sea coast the plane was caught in the beams of three searchlights and the pilot had to dive sharply to avoid the incoming flak (*Fleiger Luft Abwehr Kanone*), anti-aircraft gunfire. Shortly after the shooting stopped the message came through on the intercom, Coastal batteries. Common stuff here. It's all over now."

The dispatcher, the person who organised her parachute jump, asked her if she would be able to jump by herself. She replied that she would, but if something went wrong, he had to push her out.

At 2345 hours the plane was in position and she was ready to jump but the red light stayed on. There was no reception committee waiting for her or the containers. After almost an hour of circling the drop zone, the pilot told his crew he was returning to base. Desperately she pleaded with the dispatcher to get the pilot to do one more run as she said that she would never be able to go through such an adventure again. The pilot made one more approach. This time the signs on the ground were seen. The red light changed to green and she jumped.

In the early hours of the morning on March 10 1945, the same day that the Allies reached the River Rhine, she was parachuted at low altitude near Benthuizen, about ten miles (16 kms.) east of The Hague. The wind was strong and she injured her back when she, like Antonia, landed in a ditch.

Although the reception committee looked after her, she caught an infection which had to be treated with the penicillin she had brought with her. Once in The Hague she arranged a message to be sent to London on 13th March saying that she had arrived safely. She then went on to work with the resistance as instructed. Not being an SOE mission, there is no personal file in the National Archives. The SIS do not appear to have files on their agents. Part of her mission was to follow the Allied advance into Germany under the guise of a secretary to a businessman and to prepare post-war talks with politicians. The OSS wanted her to work with the thousands of Dutch forced labourers and Allied prisoners in German factories to encourage acts of sabotage and slow downs. This was part of Operation BONZO, a plan which involved dropping anti-Nazi German agents into Germany to give the Nazis the false impression that there was a large resistance network already in place. As relations between the two countries had broken down by then and the German army was in retreat, her mission was aborted but not before she sent back awful accounts of the treatment of foreign workers. She remained working in The Hague following instruction to demoralise the remaining Germans. During that time, conditions were still very tense.

If I felt that a rendezvous was not right, I always escaped. I went into a large department store, came down the lift and went into a restaurant or anywhere where I could be with my back against the wall to be able to see all the entrances and exits.
Once when I arrived at an appointment in Utrecht I had the feeling that something was up. I warned the two youngsters I'd met not to return to the train station, but they ignored my advice. They were both arrested and within a week they were dead. (Mulder-Gemmeke, J. 12297, IWMSA)

After crossing the Rhine at Wesel and Rees, Canadian forces liberated first the eastern and then the northern provinces of Holland. The western provinces had to wait until the retreating German forces capitulated on the evening of May 5 1945. the surrender was negotiated at the De Wereld Hotel in Wageningen. Then followed massive food drops to feed the starving population. Crews from Tempsford started their first daytime drops into Holland. At 2301 hours on 8 May, war was over.

Afterwards Jos was awarded one of the country's highest honours, a medal of the *Militaire Willemsorde*, the Military Order of William. She kept as souvenirs her pistol, her flask of Cognac drink which she drank to mitigate the impact of her jump, a compass and the belt which held the hundred thousand guilders she had brought for the resistance movement.

A suitable postscript comes from Foot's comprehensive account of Dutch resistance during the war. Whilst not mentioning names, it is worth remembering the work of some Dutch women in their eventual success.

A vast amount of undercover work was done by the Dutch resisters, as it had been done in the autumn by Belgian, as the advance swept forward from the Wesel toward the Baltic: providing up-to-the-minute information on where the enemy was and what he was doing, mopping up parties not disposed of by the main advance, guarding - eventually, herding - prisoners, preserving bridges and locks. 'In nearly all the liberated towns and villages', SOE's reports for the week ending 15 April (1945) *remarked, 'order has been maintained by Resistance leaders who have taken control of their respective area.* (Foot, op.cit. p.423)

Appendix

1. SCHREIDER'S 100 QUESTIONS

Sturmbannfuhrer (Major) Joseph Schreieder, the head of counter-espionage and counter-sabotage in Holland, following the war, provided a list of the questions he wanted his interrogators to ask their captured SOE and SIS agents. They indicate just how exhaustively they questioned the early captives and what information they had managed to extricate about the inner workings of the British secret services. It needs to be added that the British interrogators very likely used exactly the same type of questions to captured German agents.

1. Length of stay in ENGLAND before the agent set out on his mission
2. Had the agent fled from HOLLAND or where did he originally come from?
3. To which Resistance Organisation did he belong in Holland?
4. What position did he hold in the organisation and what were his duties?
5. Why did he escape from HOLLAND?
6. When did he escape?
7. Name, description, last and probable present residence of refugees, who might, even if only temporarily, have gone with him.
8. Detailed description of escape route.
9. In which transit camps for refugees did he stay on his journey?
10. Did he meet any persons known to him in any of these camps?
11. What organisations or individuals aided him in his flight, either financially or by other means, e.g. providing him with

contacts, etc?

12. When did he arrive in ENGLAND?

13. To which or by what British or Dutch officials did he report or was he expected on arrival? (Name and address of such officials and location of such offices including a description of the personnel employed there.)

14. Did he meet any Dutch or other refugees whom he knew personally at these places?

15. Did the agent, before being sent to a screening camp (Ueberprüfungslager), come into contact with any officials other than those he had reported to or was met by in the first place?

16. Name and location of screening camp. (Was it under English or Dutch supervision?)

17. Length of stay at the screening camp.

18. How many people of Dutch or other nationality lived in such a camp?

19. Did he personally know any of the inmates of the camp? If so, name, address and probable permanent residence.

20. Who interrogated him?

21. What questions were put to him?

22. Place of residence and occupation after he left the screening camp.

23. When, where, by whom and under what circumstances was he asked to become an agent?

24. When and where did he agree to become and sign on as an agent? (British or Dutch Office?)

25. What other persons, there for the same purpose, did he meet on that occasion? (Name, description, residence.)

26. After signing on, was he at once sent to a school for agents, or was he given a place to live in (flat, house) and told to await further orders? (Name and location of school or residence.)

27. Names and descriptions of any other persons with whom he

shared a flat or house, during the waiting period.
28. Were these people also waiting for further orders?
29. When was he first sent to an agents' school?
30. How and through whom did he get his orders?
31. By what means and by whom was he taken to the school? Was he taken to the school alone or did he travel with others?

> The number of schools attended by the agent were to be given in chronological order and for each school the following points had to be covered:

33. Name and/or number of school.
34. Name of town, village, etc.
35. Other details of location.
36. Description of school building (external appearance, internal layout).
37. Name and description of Commander in Chief and instructors. What subjects were taught by individual instructors?
38. The name under which the agent was known at the school.
39. Number and names of his co-pupils (real name, any alias, nickname, term of endearment or school name). Description of his co-pupils. What does the agent know about the individual pupils?
40. Did he get to know members of any other course?
41. Details of school curriculum.
42. What was taught in each subject?
43. What were the practical exercises like?
44. What apparatus or materials were used for such exercises?
45. Give the daily routine from reveille to Lights-out.
46. Length of time spent in each school.

47. Was the agent conveyed from school to school singly or with other pupils? Id so, names.
48. Who was in charge of such transport?
49. Where did the agent live in the intervals between courses (schooling) if one course did not immediately follow the other.
50. If any of his co-pupils left in the middle of a course or did not arrive at the next school, give their possible employment.
51. Give the description as in No. 39 of any newcomers to the school.
52. Where did the agent live after completion of schooling and before going on operations? (If he did not stay at a Holding School.)
53. Which other agents lived with him?
54. With which British or Dutch authorities or officials did the agent come into contact before going on ops?
55. When and who handed the agent his written operation orders? When and to whom did he return these orders after learning them by heart?
56. Repeat verbatim such orders (orders to be written out by the agent by hand in the second person.)
57. Did the agent have any knowledge of the orders given to other agents?
58. In connection with the first part of the agent's mission, did he get any addresses of contacts in HOLLAND?
59. Were agents supplied with contacts outside HOLLAND and if so, why?
60. Name and description of agents with whom he was to work. Were the latter already at work or were they to be dropped with him?
61. Date on which he commenced operations.
62. Had the agent been dropped or had he been sent ashore from a boat? (The latter method was no longer in use after April 1942.)

63. Were British or Dutch officers or any other people present at the farewell dinner?
64. Name and description of any agent at these farewell dinners. (When did they go on operations?)
65. Who took the agent to the starting point?
Which other agents started the same evening in other aircraft? (Names, descriptions.)

NOTE: There were no questions about the name or location of the airfield out of which they were flown.

67. Does the agent know about the operational use of other agents?
68. Cover-name used by the agent while on board the aircraft.
69. Name, description and mission of other agents travelling on the same aircraft.
70. Exact time of start.
71. When and where were the agents dropped?
72. When and where and with whom had the agent been dropped?
73. Were any WT (Wireless Transmission) or DF (Direction Finding) sets dropped and where are they now?
74. If these sets were not used by the agent or agents, for whom were they intended.
75. Was it part of the duty of the agent or agents to deliver letters or parcels (disguised objects) to addresses given to him in ENGLAND?
76. Was the agent received in the dropping area?
77. What passwords did he have to exchange with the person who met him?
78. What was the text of his message reporting his successful landing? Did such a message have a check (control)?
79. How was the report sent? By pigeon or by W/T?

80. Where was the agent taken after he landed?
81. Where were any others taken after he landed?
82. Name used on the agent's personal pass.
83. Names used on other agents' personal passes.
84. Name used by the agent and his assistants in the WT messages.
85. Did the agent have a WT operator with him or did he transmit himself? In the first case di the agent have his own code?
86. Number and make of WT sets.
87. Name and location of the transmission site. Next time for transmission.
88. Brief description of basic code used (book-code, poetry-code, transposition tables, etc.).
89. Brief description of other coding methods used by the agent (letter code, Playfair, Platzbestimmung).
90. The possible use of an agent's number or key cipher (Detailed interrogation on WT technicalities and ciphers was done by officials of the *Orpo (Ordnungspolizei*) and *Kriminaloberseketär)* MAY-Controls.)
91. How much money did the agent or agents carry and for what purpose was the money to be used?
92. Did the agent or agents receive any orders other than the written orders?
93. What did the agent do until his arrest and what part of his mission had he accomplished?
94. Had the agent collaborated with any resistance organisation and to what did his collaboration amount?
95. What channels for contacting his assistant were used by the agent and how could he get hold of his assistant in case of emergency?
96. Number and contents of WT messages sent and received by the agent until his arrest. (Who drafted and encoded these

messages?)
97. Name and description of any other agents whom he met after he had been dropped. (How could he get in touch with them?)
98. Did the agent contact any of his relations? E.g. parents, wife?
With whom, where and at what time has the agent appointments which he has not yet fulfilled?
Has the agent or his assistant received orders to return to ENGLAND within a certain time, or is he expecting someone from there? (Appendix 5 in Michael Foot's *SOE in the Low Countries*, (2001), St Ermin's Press, pp.503-508)

2. STENTOR MISSION FOR THE NETHERLANDS

Preface

Events in France have shown the paramount necessity for ensuring a dependable means of keeping in touch with the individual people in the occupied countries, so that they may receive not only the Directives which the Allied High Command may from time to time wish to give them, but also daily information on events in general.

It has, in the past, largely fallen to the Clandestine Press to disseminate the truth to all loyal and resisting Netherlanders, but as speed now becomes an important factor additional means must be devised.

It is consequently desired to organise a system of listening groups throughout the country, which s will be seen later, should be self-contained in so far as the reception and dissemination of news and directives is concerned.

To accomplish this task you will require the collaboration of reliable organisers to whom it will be your duty to explain exactly what is required.

It is thought that the country should be organised on the basis of provinces and that a separate organiser should be placed in charge of such divisions. It will be for you to decide how such a division is to be made and how many organisers will be required for the purpose. Some provinces, by virtue of their particular conformation, density of population etc., may require an individual organiser, whilst others may be placed together under similar control.

The key-notes which it is desired to strike are those of decentralisation in organisation and rapidity in dissemination.

Certain supplementing objectives can be assigned to the listening groups which it is desired to establish notably: -

To counteract enemy propaganda and to destroy the effect and value of false information, directives and rumours circulated by him.

Generally to demoralise the enemy himself and all quislings.

Having made your division of the country on the lines indicated and selected your organisers - who incidentally, with the object of decentralisation in mind, should not be known to each other personally as fulfilling complementary roles - you will brief them on the lines of the mission attached hereto.

In its successful and speedy establishment lie the means of speeding the liberation of your country and safeguarding your resisting compatriots. Good luck.

ORGANISATION OF THE PROVINCE/S

To ascertain in the province/s assigned to you what dependable listening groups already exist, and to increase their number by the inclusion of as many additional trustworthy patriots as possible, and to extend their operations daily throughout the twenty-four hours. You will, consequently, make your own preliminary organisation, which should include such a listening group, before you approach one of the established resistance organisations for support, as it is felt that you are more likely to carry weight if your organisation itself is already in being.

In order to proceed as quickly as possible you will enlist as many reliable assistants as necessary, and after briefing them on the lines herein, you will allot each a definite sub-territory, which they will in turn organise and administer on identical lines. To achieve the essential object of decentralisation, such sub-organisers should not be known to each other, though it is appreciated that this counsel of perfection will not always be attainable.

Your object in a few words will be to organise all sectors until the whole of your territory from towns down to the smallest villages, are covered, though here again, this ideal is not likely to be fully achieved in practice.

It is anticipated that a number of listening posts already functioning through main sets may not be available later, and you will therefore provide for the inclusion of as many battery posts as possible.

Plans should be made for these battery posts to be adequately screened, if necessary by removal from one point to another in any given section.

In short it is desired to ensure that whatever combination of circumstances may arise, no organised sector will be cut off from contact with LONDON, or is vulnerable to infiltration by the enemy.

As regards the provision of batteries, and/or battery sets, we can supply these at your request.

<u>THE DISSEMINATION OF INFORMATION AND DIRECTIVES</u>

Your task under this heading will be to ensure that as wide a range of publicity as possible is given to all directives and information received by the listening posts. The methods which it is anticipated you will use are as follows: -

> *Graffiti, hand written, typed, roneo'd and printed tracts and posters. Oral dissemination of news and directives should not be relied upon as it leads to mutilation, though it should of course be used where necessary and particularly to counteract rumours.*

Arrangements for the dissemination as specified above should be carried out through suitable cut-outs, by listening posts themselves. The object to be achieved here is to ensure that each individual listening group is capable of immediately disseminating over as wide a territory as possible the news and directives which it receives. If for any reason a listening group should break down, it should place its dissemination service at the disposal of some other group in the vicinity.

A very considerable measure of success would be achieved if it were possible for each listening group to organise for a daily news sheet to be exhibited in some public place/s in towns and villages, etc.

3. <u>TO COUNTERACT AND DESTROY FALSE INFORMATION</u>

False information will be counteracted by the wide dissemination of the true facts. Here the methods in 2.

(a) will be relied upon.

The one reliable antidote to all rumour is the truth and every opportunity should, therefore, be taken to pull down enemy posters; to mutilate them if this is impossible, and to destroy all enemy tracts. The public should be educated to test all information which it receives. Firstly, is the information itself of such a character as, by its dissemination, to harm the Allies, and benefit the enemy? Secondly is it vouched for by someone they know has received it first hand?

TO DEMORALISE THE ENEMY

This is best effected by the following means:-

Dissemination of the truth as described in 3 above.

Tracts in German, not necessarily black, giving important news items from the fronts should be printed. Allied victories and successes emphasised etc.

Dissemination of Black German propaganda when procurable.

By all acts calculated to make the occupying enemy forces additionally conscious of the fact that they are amongst a hostile population. Ingenuity and local circumstances will suggest the form that such acts should take, but in general, they should not be of such a nature as to endanger the risk of reprisals, though as events develop in favour of the Allies, bolder and more far-reaching action will be possible with diminishing risk.

OUTLINE OF INSTRUCTIONS FOR AGENTS

Every possible opportunity of educating the local population for the purpose of liberation and stimulating their determination to be rid of their oppressors should be seized.

Your help is asked along the lines shown below but without interfering with your main tasks. Remember in carrying out any of these activities it is of the utmost importance that neither your specific mission nor any local resistance organisation should be jeopardised.

Those who are not specialists acting on specific instructions, must conserve their energies and their organisations for the day when the Supreme Allied Commander will tell them when and how in the best interests of themselves and of the military situation they should act. That order will be given.

Seek rather to recruit and train trustworthy colleagues to carry out the work involved.

Your main role is to provide the direction and leadership without which many vitally important tasks may be left undone.

NEWS

The ENEMY's chief weapon against civilians, as in 1940, will be rumour and false news. Therefore try to arrange now that the facts about any landings will reach the people through persons they know they can trust. See to it that the people are constantly warned and reminded about the danger of acting upon news from any other source.

Organise a regular listening service to Allied radio broadcasts

Publish this news as regularly as possible

Even if the news cannot be printed or duplicated it can be passed on by word of mouth.

Appoint trustworthy local people to serve

as channels for news and to stamp out rumours.

INSTRUCTIONS TO THE CIVIL POPULATION FROM ALLIED HIGH COMMAND

A major handicap to the enemy during invasion is a civilian population working against the GERMANS in full accordance with instructions issued from LONDON by radio. Therefore, see to it that instructions intended for the civilian population reach them without delay, through an organised news service.

Apart from any specific instructions you now have or general ones to be issued, attention to any or all of the following operations will be of vital importance in the period of liberation:

SAFEGUARD LOYAL SPECIALIST OR KEY SERVICE PERSONNEL

Register, collect, hide and safeguard: -
Radio announcers and transmission engineers
Press editors and newspaper printing specialists
Morse operators
Gas, electricity, water, sewage, railway, tramway, telephone, factory and mine engineers
Dockers, road menders, M.T. mechanics

The absence of these specialists will weaken the ENEMY while their assistance when the liberating armies reach the district will be invaluable.

B. OBSTRUCT ENEMY AND QUISLING ADMINISTRATION

a) Exert pressure on traitors in possession of key information or in administrative key positions: -

i) to disclose knowledge of ENEMY counter-invasion plans, including police arrangements, movements or concentrations of troops or war materials, food stocks etc.

ii) to delay and obstruct administrative machinery.

b) You can undermine the position of the GERMANS and collaborators in various ways: -

i) No chance should be missed in making mischief between the GERMANS and the collaborators by spreading false trails which may lead to denunciations and recriminations.

ii) Attempts should be made to build up the hope among minor collaborators and GERMANS that by handing over the important collaborators and GERMANS to the Allies or the liberated local authorities they may escape punishment, and that in the meantime they can help insure their positions by surreptitiously aiding resistance.

iii) Spread the slogan that he who does not now actively prove himself on the side of the Allies will afterwards be assumed to have been against them.

c) You should keep careful watch on all GERMAN preparations, particularly for demolitions, and on troop movements and be in a position to help Allied forces.

d) In order to prevent destruction of food and the GERMANS seizing and carrying it away in their retreat, supplies of food must be scattered as much as possible in small quantities, and not allowed to accumulate in large dumps.

C. <u>UNDERMINE ENEMY TROOP MORALE</u>
Use any means to depress and unnerve ENEMY troops such as: -

Circulation of news about military events with emphasis on details of GERMAN losses in the theatre of war

Circulation of news about ALLIED bombing operations against GERMAN troops

Irritation and exasperation of local GERMAN troops with a view to producing bad discipline. (TNA HS 6/767)

Bibliography

Binney, M. (2003), *The Women Who Lived For Danger*, William Morrow

Burton, C. (Winter 2005) 'The Eureka-Rebecca compromises: another look at special operations security during World War II', *Air Power History*

Clark, F. (1999), *Agents by Moonlight*, Tempus Publishing

Deacon, R. (1969), *The History of the British Secret Service*, Frederick Muller, London

de Roever, E. (1985), *Zij sprongen bij maanlicht: de geschiedenis van het Bureau Bijzondere Opdrachten en de agenten*, p. 136. Baarn, Hollandia

de Roever, E. (1987), *Sphinx: het verhaal van Jos Gemmeke*, Hollandia Publishers, Baarn,

Eman, D. (1999), *Things We Couldn't Say*, Wm. B. Eerdman's Publishing Company

Escott, B. (1991), *Mission Improbable, A Salute to the RAF Women of SOE in Wartime France*, Sparkford: Patrick Stephens Limited

Foot, M.R.D. (2001), *The SOE in the Low Countries*, St Ermin's Press

Gemeke-Mulder, J. What I did during the war, was no heroism, *Elsevier Magazine*, May 2009

Hastings, M. 'Winston Churchill the Terrorist', *Daily Mail*, 21 August 2009

Neave, A. (1969), *Saturday at MI9*, Hodder and Stoughton

Oliver, D. (2005), *Airborne Espionage*, The History Press Ltd.

Smith, G. (1999), *Cambridgeshire Airfields in the Second World War*, Countryside Books, Newbury, p. 271

Verity, H. (1998), *We Landed by Moonlight*, Crecy Publishing

Jo Wolters, 'Remarks Concerning a Research Note on *The Dutch Affair*', *Intelligence and National Security* 21, no. 3 (Jun. 2006): 459-466

Documents
National Archives HS 6/762 CHICORY (Jos Gemmeke)
National Archives HS 6/767 Antonia and Frank Hamilton
National Archives HS 9/1452/8 Beatrice Trix Terwindt

Websites
http://www.chicheleyhall.co.uk/
http://www.deborahjackson.net/childrensnovels/timemeddlersundercover/specialoperationsexecutive.html
www.dbnl.org
http://www.englandspiel.eu/introductie.php?taal=en http://www.fpp.co.uk/History/General/SOEHolland.html
http://www.leerwiki.nl/De_enige_nog_levende_vrouw_met_de_Militaire_Willems_Orde
http://www.nisa-intelligence.nl/PDF-bestanden/KluitersDAGversie2.pdf
http://nl.wikipedia.org/wiki/Jos_Gemmeke
http://www.onderscheidingenforum.nl/viewtopic.php?f=24&t=776
http://www.oorlogsgetuigen.nl/Silence/
http://static.rnw.nl/migratie/www.wereldomroep.nl/actua/nl/nederland/geschiedenis/herdenkingspecial/verzet040504.html-redirected
http://vlex.com/vid/eureka-rebecca-compromises-operations-ii-56727120
http://www.ww2awards.com/person/341

www.ingramcontent.com/pod-product-compliance
Lightning Source LLC
Chambersburg PA
CBHW071825090426
42737CB00012B/2182

* 9 7 8 1 9 0 2 8 1 0 3 6 2 *